s, Hoffman Reynolds.
    Explorers of man; five pioneers in anthropology [by]
. R. Hays. New York, Crowell-Collier Press [1971]

    218 p.   ports.   24 cm.   $5.95

    CONTENTS.—Henry Rowe Schoolcraft.—Adolph Bastian.—Broni-
slaw Malinowski.—Claude Lévi-Strauss.—Margaret Mead.—Bibliog-
raphy (p. [209]-211)


    1. Anthropologists—Juvenile literature.   [1. Anthropologists]
I. Title.

GN20.H38                                                70-135645
                        301.29'22   [B]   [920]
                                                        MARC
Library of Congress              71 [25-2]              A C

# EXPLORERS OF MAN

# H. R. HAYS

# EXPLORERS OF MAN

## FIVE PIONEERS IN ANTHROPOLOGY

CROWELL-COLLIER PRESS, NEW YORK

Library of Congress Catalog Card Number: 70–135645

The Macmillan Company
866 Third Avenue
New York, New York 10022

Collier-Macmillan Canada Ltd., Toronto, Ontario

Printed in the United States of America

10   9   8   7   6   5   4   3   2   1

PICTURE CREDITS
Black Star, 140; Culver Pictures, Inc., 14, 62;
Radio Times Hulton Picture Library, 104;
United Press International, 172.

# CONTENTS

# INTRODUCTION

This book deals with the life and work of five outstanding scholars in the field of anthropology. Among them we find two Americans, a German, an anglicized Pole and a Frenchman, a distribution which is fairly typical of the variety of contributions made by different nations to this study. Since the four men and one woman will be discussed in historical order, their work will serve as a sample of what has been done in the field since investigation first began.

Anthropology is derived from two Greek words, man and word, meaning, of course, the study of man. It was not until fairly recently that man undertook the study of himself. The reason for this is that only with the development of western science has a sense of objectivity arisen which has made it possible to look in the mirror. In earlier times, in Greece or in the Middle Ages, the human animal took himself for granted as unique. The world was made for him and he was the center of the universe except for supernatural forces, shaped in his own image, which set an ideal pattern for his life. The discovery that the sun did not revolve around the earth was the turning point; from then on human pride was reduced. As the science of astronomy progressed, the world diminished to a whirling dot in a vast universe; our group of planets was merely one of many galaxies. With this came the suspicion that man was perhaps not the only intelligent being in existence.

From the self-centered position, human beings were able to admire each other, enslave each other, write poetry about each other, deplore each other's sins, threaten each other with divine punishment and conclude they deserved immortality. They did not consider each other objects for study. Advances in the sciences of biology and zoology, however, showed more and more clearly that man had much in common with other living beings. He had a heart that beat, his veins and arteries could be compared to the circulatory systems of other animals. The same was true of his nervous system, digestive apparatus and means of reproduction. The study of embryology showed that from the coming together of two cells all kinds of living forms had developed, including man himself. And, Oh horrors! his anatomy was not unlike that of the larger apes.

Gradually the mysteries of human biology, the complicated mechanisms of the body began to be better understood. And if the body could be studied as if it were a machine, why not the mind? And if there could be a science of the mind, why not one of human behavior?

But what is human behavior? Everything a man does, or makes, or thinks is part of his behavior. It becomes clear that we cannot sketch a definition of the study of man in a couple of words.

Historically it all began when the European, who considered himself the supreme achievement of civilization, started to take a somewhat patronizing interest in people living in much simpler material societies. Indeed the line between the animal and the human was not clear to early zoologists. Such eighteenth-century naturalists as the Frenchman Georges Buffon recorded travellers' tales of talking apes. Because of original sin, had some people degenerated to a degraded condition?

When Captain Cook encountered the Hawaiians in 1778, he had already landed on several South Sea archipelagos and observed peoples who were handsome and beautifully built, who wore few clothes, had strange ideas about marriage and worshipped various types of gods. The good captain noted down these facts in his journals and included such customs as that of *kapu* or magical prohibition adhered to by the Hawaiians. It was kapu for Hawaiian women and men to eat together because the bad magic of the woman would affect the man.

It was just such unusual customs which gave an initial impetus to the study of anthropology. Starting from idle curiosity, scholarly men began to wonder why people in different places looked different and behaved so differently. Finally they were fascinated to discover coherent systems of thought behind unfamiliar acts. Eventually they were led to wonder if such habits bore some relation to those of civilized men. Were there historical developments in human society which could be traced from early times? Was the sequence a matter of increasing complexity? How did certain beliefs or practices spread all over the world? By the comparative study of human societies could we decide what was useful and good and what ought to be scrapped?

At the same time that these studies were beginning, a blend of anatomical investigation and zoological science was brought to bear on man's physical attributes. Attempts to define so-called races were given a new impetus by the discovery of ancient fossil skeletons or parts of skeletons which displayed characteristics differing from those of modern man. Eventually, after much opposition, the presence of these fossils was accepted as proof that man had not always existed in the form of a European university professor. The famous Neanderthal type, first discovered in 1856, left no art or ornaments and probably wore no clothes. It was conveniently decided that he died out or was exterminated and modern man was descended from the better-looking and generally more satisfactory Cro-Magnon type. Nowadays, however, there are scholars who believe that the Neanderthal never died out, probably mixed with other strains and, if he were alive today, could interbreed with contemporary humans, and, if dressed, could pass unnoticed in a crowd.

Humility is the father of objectivity in the study of man, and anthropologists, with the passage of time, have steadily driven home the fact that the human race enjoys no special privileges other than those accruing to him from his own (often unapplied) intelligence.

To return to the definition of anthropology, it did in fact gradually split into two main branches: physical and social or cultural anthropology.

Until recent decades, physical anthropology has stuck fast in the rather static activity of classification. The old notion was that races were separately created but that intermediates had occurred from racial mixtures. Scholars assumed that their task was description and could be carried out by setting up racial traits. Since length and width of heads was supposed to be a basic characteristic, for years physical anthropologists went about measuring heads with large calipers. Eventually the idea of race acquired so many political, emotional and thoroughly unscientific overtones that the term should be used rarely and with extreme caution. Since all of mankind is one species, it is best to speak of human varieties. Physical anthropology continues to busy itself with the development of man's biological characteristics and the distribution of types. The development and origin of the human species in a zoological sense is also within its province.

Social anthropology, on the other hand, in terms of the word social, deals with what happens between people. These relationships are affected by what the group considers to be proper behavior and can therefore be handed down from one generation to the next. When behavior changes, this, too, is significant and interesting.

In other words, if we discover that a certain tribe believes that five wives is the proper number for a chief to marry, we now know something about the institution of marriage. Immediately new questions arise, some of which we will be able to answer by further study. Why did the tribe pick the number five? How long have they had this rule? How many wives do the common people have? What is the status of women under this system? Did the tribe originate the rule or did they borrow it from some other group? Do the chiefs really stick to the rules or in real life do they have four or six wives? Does this rule seem to work well for this particular people? Does the number five have magical significance and turn up in other institutions? Are there religious myths which proclaim the number five sacred? Finally, and this sort of question is not often asked but it should be more frequently, is our western formula of one wife to one man better or worse for the human community?

I have here picked an imaginary marriage situation as an example, but every activity carried on by a group of people undergoes the scrutiny of the study of man.

Now this leads us to an important point. If the study of man deals with everything he does, then anthropology must overlap other sciences. As we have seen, when we look at man as an animal, zoology and biology come into the picture. The investigation of his past achievements, without which we cannot understand the present, takes us into history and prehistory. Since we are deeply concerned with his mental and emotional processes we cannot operate without help from the science of psychology. How he gets his living shapes his acts and this brings us to the study of economics. A man's language is often the key to much of his behavior and so we must call upon the study of linguistics to understand why he says what he says. Oral poetry and myths, of course, tell us a great deal about his view of the world and his justification of why he does what he does. And so immediately we are involved in literary criticism, not to mention art criticism, when we study the images he carves on his paddles and war clubs. And, if he has any coherent system of ideas about the world and his place in it we are led to religion and philosophy. Finally, we try to see the relationships between all of these areas if we are to have any notion of the total picture and to understand the pattern of a culture.

For instance, an African mask will have a myth connected with it, is in itself an artistic object, will be used in certain ritual behavior which has religious significance. It will be made and handled by certain people who may be witch doctors or not, will, in its shape, reflect its creator's ideas about humans and animals, will probably be handed down in a family and thus be connected with property values and very likely certain persons will not be allowed to look at it for magical reasons. We see then that social anthropology should ideally involve a complete understanding of all the relationships between people in groups and between their institutions. In practice we do not achieve this but it is worth a try.

I mentioned the fact earlier that social anthropology is sometimes called cultural anthropology. The distinction here gets rather tricky. The dictionary will not help us much since it first defines *a culture* as a complex (or collection) of kinds of behavior and when we look up *a society* we are eventually referred back to the definition of a culture. Scholars, however, do seem to have some distinction in their minds when they speak of one or the other. Perhaps there is a tendency to think of society as composed of actual individuals living in a group of thatched huts while they thread their way through the maze of habits, regulations and daily chores (carefully avoiding their mothers-in-law because to speak to them is magically dangerous) all of which constitutes their culture. The image might be something like that of red blood cells moving around in plasma and adjusting their shape as they go through smaller blood vessels and negotiate curves and bends.

Some anthropologists attempt to separate human beings from culture. To them culture is some magical abstraction produced by human society and they seem to believe that it is governed by laws like physics or mathematics. Whether there are definable laws or not, it seems clear that a habit or a custom began somewhere and that an individual had something to do with it. And thus culture and society are intertwined.

As may be seen we have gotten this far in our definition of social anthropology by walking around it, indicating some of the things it isn't and by listing some of the things it does. There is perhaps one more important distinction which has to be thrashed out. What is the difference between anthropology and the closely related study of sociology? Once again, like that between society and culture, there is definitely an overlap. Once again, dictionary definitions are similar with the exception that that of anthropology is broader. Actually one of the great founders of sociology, the French scholar, Émile Durkheim, can also be considered to be an anthropologist. Also, in 1921, two sociologists, Robert and Helen Lynd, made a study of a midwestern city which they called Middletown, in which they approached the town exactly as if it were a primitive tribe and endeavored to sketch a complete picture of its institutions.

Up to that time it could be said that sociology tended to deal with contemporary groups while anthropology had tended to seek out the preliterates. On the whole it is true that sociological studies tend to be concerned with limited, isolated problems and to rely a good deal on a statistical approach. The famous Kinsey report, *Sexual Behavior in the Human Male*, is an example of this approach, while an early classic, *The Life of a South African Tribe*, by Henri Junod, might be used as a contrasting type of anthropological study. Kinsey used questionnaires and brief interviews and tabulated the results statistically. He was concerned with the sex habits of American men and nothing else. His critics would say that the people he chose for his poll were perhaps not truly representative of the nation and that many did not answer the questionnaires honestly and fully. Junod, on the other hand, relied partly on his own observations, since he lived among his Africans for years. He was thus also able to judge the value of the information he got by asking questions because he knew the characters of his informants. His aim was to paint a picture of the life of the tribe and all its institutions and he filled in the details by putting down what he saw happening about him. The criticism of his approach would be that everything he recorded was filtered through his own personality. His particular prejudices and moral judgements may have distorted the picture and prevented him from fully understanding what he saw and heard. Social anthropologists have all along been more literary and more fun to read than sociologists. They have been interested in the shape of culture and in trying to put things together rather than taking them apart. In other words, anthropologists have often displayed some of the talents of a good novelist in capturing peoples' reactions to each other, something that no statistical tables can ever achieve.

Whatever culture is, it does not stand still. Someone invents an automobile and from then on boys and girls go out alone together without an elderly spy who used, in the nineteenth century, to be called a chaperone. Similarly a missionary gives steel axes to the women of an Australian tribe in which stone axes were used exclusively by men. This simple act cuts the underpinning from the whole social system, the men lose their authority, the young people lose their guidelines for living and the whole tribe undergoes cultural shock and dies out. Or an energetic and warlike tribe, which we have come to call the Incas, conquers all the other tribes living on the spine of the Andes and on parts of the coast, and forces all the subject peoples to worship the sun. These are a few of the ways in which society and/or culture is continually changed. Strangely enough, it took anthropologists quite a long time before they realized that they must take change into account. Their first attempts were conditioned by the mentality of the museum curator, they wanted to pin down and classify cultural traits and institutions.

Anthropology rather than sociology has studied the history of culture. Early in the nineteenth century, when the ideas of Darwin were popular, it was thought that a scheme or map could be worked out to show how "lower" forms of behavior gradually evolved into "higher" ones. Polygyny, the possession of many wives, was supposed to give way to the higher concept of one wife, just as many gods were thought to be abandoned in favor of one. A greater variety of material from many areas has since destroyed the idea that any one simple pattern will cover the past history of man.

Another problem attacked by early anthropologists was that of distribution of cultural traits. A particular group of scholars, who seemed to think that preliterates were rather stupid, felt that inventions were made only once. In Polynesia, a wooden headrest that fits under the neck as a pillow is widespread. Something very similar is used in Japan but it also turns up in Africa. Does this mean that all these people had contact with one another and that the headrest spread from a central source? Undoubtedly there is borrowing through trade and as a result of the conquest of one people by another. Migrations of various groups also account for the spread of objects and customs. An opposing school of thought, however, suggested that peoples' minds worked in similar ways all over the world and consequently, given certain practical needs and certain environmental situations, similar solutions would result. For instance, at a seashore, lake or river, people would all tend to make nets and fishhooks to catch fish, only they would make them of different materials. There was no reason why these gimmicks could not be invented again and again.

Another interesting distribution problem occurred in the appearance of certain mythological themes in various parts of the world. For instance, the flood story is familiar to us from the Bible but it is also present in Sumerian and Babylonian literature before the Hebrew version. It is easy to say that it was sparked by a local flooding of the Euphrates river. But stories of the destruction of the world by fire and flood occur in the South Seas and also in North American Indian literature and are particularly wonderful and vivid in the sacred literature of the Mayas of Central America and the Aztecs of Mexico. The Indian peoples of the Americas came over from Asia ten or fifteen thousand years ago or perhaps even further back in history. It seems unlikely that they could have carried with them the memory of some primal flood.

Since, except in limited areas, not much could be proved concerning distribution without a great deal more data, these diffusionist arguments gradually died out. Only recently, however, a very controversial writer, Immanuel Velikovsky, has come up with the claim that the earth was struck by a comet around 1500 B.C., and that the memory of fire and floods, destruction and darkness in the literature and legends of so many people reflects this catastrophic event which damaged the whole world. Most scientists do not think that Velikovsky has yet proved his case but he does assemble, in his chapters on primitive literature, a remarkably challenging array of evidence.

We have indicated some of the major areas with which social anthropology is concerned. How did the actual science begin? What were some of the first steps it took? Actually many of the earliest scholars were what might be called armchair anthropologists. They compiled books from material reported by other people without themselves ever meeting any of the people they wrote about. As we have said, eighteenth century explorers, such as Cook and his contemporary, Louis Comte de Bougainville, who landed on the island of Tahiti in 1766, were one type of source. Then there were the missionaries who sometimes modified their attitude of disapproval long enough to set down some notes on the inhabitants' customs. In Canada, the Jesuits, such as Joseph François LaFitau, who wrote in 1724, were pioneer students of the North American Indians. In southern Mexico, the Spanish bishop Diego de Landa burned all the Indian texts as idolatrous but did at least set down some very valuable facts before he got rid of his sources. The Spanish historian, Garcilaso de la Vega, whose mother was an Inca princess, wrote a long book describing the culture of the native people of Peru. Besides these outstanding names, there was a host of hunters and travellers who had visited foreign lands from whose memoirs bits of information could be plucked.

None of the early German or English writers on cultural history were what we today would call field workers. Interestingly enough, the idea of field work has become extremely important in anthropology. A student is expected to spend some time with a particular people or tribe (generally an example of a nontechnological culture) about which he writes his doctoral dissertation. The young scholar thus learns to be objective, studies with sympathetic understanding the details of another way of life and learns tolerance. The whole experience is a kind of initiation and very often the investigator comes to identify profoundly with his or her chosen group. Indeed this prerequisite field training is perhaps what differentiates the anthropologist most sharply from the sociologist.

Field work leads us to the first important figure in our group of anthropologists since this man wrote out of an intimate knowledge of a people among whom he had lived. We can be proud that this first field anthropologist was an American. His name was Henry Rowe Schoolcraft.

# HENRY ROWE SCHOOLCRAFT

Young Henry Schoolcraft wanted two things: to go to college and to be a scientist. In 1808, both of these ambitions were unusual in a young country still in the pioneer stage. Schoolcraft's father, Lawrence, managed a glass factory in the small town of Hamilton, situated not far from Albany, New York. Henry, even as a boy, collected specimens of wild life, studied the rock formations in the glens cut by the streams near his house and applied himself to the study of Latin. Science was not his only interest, for he also wrote poetry, even publishing it in the local paper.

The glass business, however, was to stand in the way of his education. The United States was on the brink of the war of 1812. The elder Schoolcraft realized that, if war came, supplies of English glass would be cut off and the local product would boom. Just about the time when Henry could have entered Union College at Schenectady, Lawrence Schoolcraft had a disagreement with his superiors. He left the factory and raised money to set up a new concern in Vernon, a small town in Oneida county. While his father was in the process of organizing the new project, Henry was put in charge of the work at Hamilton. By the time he could move on to Vernon, he found his father had made new plans for him. Another group of financiers wanted to start a glass factory, and Henry, age sixteen, was to set it up and run it.

Pressure must have been used to induce Henry to undertake the job. Things went badly from the beginning. There was a great shortage of skilled glassblowers. Henry's ne'er-do-well brother, sent to help him, got in the way. Shipments of glass were not ready on time. By 1812, the factory was in a mess and Henry's father was writing him that another job was open in Vermont.

Lawrence Schoolcraft seems to have overestimated his twenty-year-old son. It is true that there were very few people in America at this time who understood the glass business. It is also true that Henry was studious and dependable. The mistake was in supposing that he could manage workmen much older than he.

Despite the fact that more calamities were to occur in the Vermont factory there was one bright spot. The plant was situated not far from Middlebury, and at Middlebury College there was Professor Frederick Hall who had a reputation in natural science and chemistry. Schoolcraft made glass equipment for the scientist's laboratory. Together they went on geological field trips collecting material for the college museum. The young man was allowed to perform experiments in the college laboratory under Hall's supervision.

Science, in the early nineteenth century, was not so sharply divided into different fields as it is today. Geology, the study of rocks, could lead to chemistry, and likewise the process of making glass required some knowledge of the chemicals which controlled its quality and its color. Mineralogy was actually partly chemistry, partly geology.

It was probably Hall's influence which set Schoolcraft to

preparing a truly scientific manual of glassmaking. Up to this time, the know-how of the craft had been secret rules of thumb passed on from one skilled worker to another. Henry School-craft envisioned it as a scientific technology.

Once more, however, he was faced with a crisis. On the one hand the war continued, making him feel uneasy because he was not in uniform although his father wrote that glassmaking was more important. On the other hand, the factory was oper-ating without sufficient capital. The creditors began to close in. The directors of the company tried the desperate expedient of printing bills adorned with a fine engraving of the glassworks. Of course, this kind of paper money was worth nothing. In 1815, Henry left with $1,800 of his salary still due.

His merciless father promptly put him in charge of a new factory in Keene, New Hampshire. By the next year, the war was over and the bottom fell out of the glass business. British ships arriving in New York sold panes of glass at auction to the highest bidder. Tariffs on foreign glass, to protect the local product, did not exist. The Keene factory went into bank-ruptcy and Henry Schoolcraft went home to Vernon.

What should he do? At first he turned to his glassmaking manual. By selling subscriptions ahead of time, perhaps he could finance the book and earn some money. This was a hope-less idea, considering the state of the glass industry. After having been the manager of three factories, he could scarcely apply for the job of a clerk. He was now twenty-seven, a tall, serious, round-faced young man wearing spectacles, self-educated beyond the level of most men of his age. He knew that he was destined for intellectual pursuits but it was now too late for college. Actually he was a practical chemist in a society in which there were no jobs for chemists.

Perhaps it was Governor DeWitt Clinton who was respon-sible for the next step in his career. The governor was a good friend of Henry's father and may well have tipped him off concerning the national lead mines. At this time, the lead mines were situated in western Arkansas and Missouri and were under the control of the Department of the Interior. They were apparently producing very little. Something would have to be done about them and some capable director would need to be put in charge.

Henry Schoolcraft's first trip into the wilderness was a sort of gamble. By visiting the sites of the mines, by learning all he could about them on the spot and preparing a report to present to the Department of the Interior, he hoped to be appointed director. It was a bold step, considering that Schoolcraft, who had always been a white-collar worker in a factory, was about to turn himself into a frontiersman with a rifle and a coonskin cap.

Early in March of 1818 (with only thirty dollars in his pocket), Henry reached Olean, in southwestern New York State, the embarkation point for the trip down the Allegheny River. Snow was still on the ground and he had to wait for the ice in the river to break up. He was not the only one with the same project in mind. Indeed he was lucky to get a room, for the town bulged at the seams with easterners going west. Heavy-set farmers in cowhide boots, followed by their wives with shawls over their heads and children clinging to their skirts, tramped the streets or gathered in the taverns and hotels. A sprinkling of woodsmen in buckskin shirts mingled with merchants who guarded their stock, carefully packed in bales and boxes, with which they hoped to open shops in the new territories. Then there were itinerant peddlers, packs on their backs, round fur caps on their heads, ready with a joke or a funny story. There were hawk-eyed fellows, chewing tobacco and whittling, who were always on the lookout for some hopeful speculation. They would buy and sell a wagonful of goods without moving it from the wagon, or they would bargain for a sawmill to be set up somewhere in Ohio, offering to pay in promises and dubious notes, forever attempting to inveigle whoever looked prosperous enough into putting capital into a sure thing. And, finally, there were the professional gamblers, soft-spoken, steady-eyed men wearing rings and watch-chains, their hair fashionably curled, on the lookout for the drunken yokel who could be persuaded to "fight the tiger" as the gambling game of faro was called. Mingling with these were the nondescript idlers and drifters who infest any large gathering, who got drunk, were sick, fell asleep in the snow and had to be dragged under cover to keep them from freezing.

The aftermath of the war had brought about a depression. Trade had languished, banks closed their doors, mortgages on farms were foreclosed and the landless farmers and unemployed manual workers turned their eyes to the West, hoping to make a new start. Some of the families Schoolcraft saw waiting for spring had scarcely more than a kneading trough on their backs. Children were clumsily dressed in the cast-off clothes of their parents, wearing mittens so full of holes their fingers were scarcely covered. They talked wistfully of the rich bottom land said to be waiting in Ohio, the cornfields they would plant on the prairie acres. It was an education for young Henry Schoolcraft. All of a sudden the country seemed to be on the move. The East with its trim white houses and imprisoning stone walls could no longer contain the young nation. Petty profits and New England prudence were no longer in tune with the spirit of the times.

Soon, he went aboard an ark belonging to a man named Pettibone, the first to set off down the river. These boats were great barges, thirty feet wide by sixty feet long, their gunwales only eighteen inches above the water's edge. On the flat deck, a superstructure, eight feet high, was erected, divided into rooms for sleeping, cooking and storing goods. The roof of the cabin was flat and used as a promenade. Near the bows were fastened two long oars which, by half rowing, half poling, kept the barge away from the bank. The craft depended on the swift current to carry it down the river and when it reached port, it would be broken up for the lumber it contained.

They reached Pittsburgh on Schoolcraft's birthday. Here he rode around the countryside, inspecting the coal mines and beds of iron ore. Quite rightly he decided that this area would become a great manufacturing center.

Schoolcraft boarded another ark, bound for Cincinnati, and on this voyage made a valuable contact. An Illinois senator, J. B. Thomas, was transporting a sawmill on another ark, tied to the first. It sprang a leak and was in danger of sinking. The passengers cried out it must be cut loose. Schoolcraft jumped on board and, under his leadership, he and another young man bailed desperately until the leak was safely above the water-line. The senator was delighted, invited the whole group to dinner and made a speech praising Schoolcraft's initiative.

Schoolcraft continued his trip in various small craft to Louisville, Kentucky, where he spent some time learning to use the long hunting rifle. During the last part of his trip he travelled on a barge which entered the Mississippi from the Ohio River. Here the water turned brown. The banks were composed of rich alluvial soil topped with a dense growth of trees and creepers and were continually undermined by the swift current. Every now and then, with a thunderous boom, great masses of earth and trees would crash into the stream, sometimes endangering the barge.

At Potosi, thirty or forty wooden houses surrounded by rolling wooded hills, he inspected his first Arkansas mines. These were leased to neighboring farmers who worked them in their spare time. Since practically no capital had been invested in equipment, out of forty mines only four or five had regular shafts but these never penetrated over eight feet and there were no proper galleries with braces and ventilation. There were no horses or engines to work pumps and, in consequence, some were flooded and abandoned. A tangle of grapevines and cottonwood covered their mouths.

With one companion and a horse to carry a pack saddle, Schoolcraft next travelled through the Ozarks, where wolves howled around the travellers at night. The two young men went down the Arkansas River in a dugout canoe, returning to Potosi by February.

Schoolcraft wrote his report on the mines, sent a letter to Senator Thomas, who he hoped might be helpful in Washington, packed up his mineral specimens and took the Mississippi steamer to New Orleans. On this boat, he met some government scientists who had been sent to explore the headwaters of the Mississippi. They told him that John C. Calhoun, the secretary of war, was particularly interested in science. He decided to keep this in mind and took passage on the brig *Arethusa* from New Orleans to New York.

When he returned to New York in August, he had made a six-thousand-mile circuit of the United States which, in his day, only reached to the Mississippi.

He stayed in New York long enough to meet a number of scholars, such as Dr. David Hosak, a professor at Columbia University, and the Yale professor, Benjamin Silliman, both students of natural history and both interested in his animal and mineral specimens, the first to be brought east from the Mississippi Valley.

Schoolcraft, bronzed and toughened by his trip, was filled with pride at being accepted by these authorities as a fellow scientist. He was proving that he could make his way in the world, even without a college degree. All this, however, did not provide him with a way of making a living. From glassmaker to mineralogist, to natural scientist, events were pushing him in a certain direction, although he was the last person in the world to have any premonition of the new field of study he would practically invent.

Washington, after New York, seemed an unfinished city. Except for the White House and a handful of public buildings, there was little indication of the classical capitol it would eventually become. Pennsylvania Avenue, its most important street, was unpaved and when it rained, carriages and horses' hooves churned the mud into a slippery mess in which pedestrians had to splash ankle-deep. The people were a curious mixture. Some had come to look for work or on government business, others to see the sights and the celebrities. Westerners in coarse hunting coats, leggings and cowhide boots mingled with southern planters in richly embroidered waistcoats, wearing carefully brushed beaver hats. There were farmers in stained homespun, long unkempt hair flowing over their collars, even Indian chiefs in beads and feathers who had come to present some petition to President Monroe.

Schoolcraft had his own interview with the president, who must have been impressed with the serious-minded young man who spoke so carefully and accurately of what he had seen on his travels. President Monroe, however, was concerned with the argument over the extension of slavery, in which Missouri was one of the key points of dissension. Monroe did not want to sign a proposed bill restricting the spread of slavery to the Missouri Territory because he was a southerner. With such matters on his mind, he was politely noncommittal concerning Schoolcraft's proposals about the Missouri lead mines.

From then on the ambitious young man was faced with the delays of government red tape, the interminably slow decision-making of government bureaus and, above all, the heart-breaking problem of getting a bill through Congress.

William Crawford, secretary of the interior, told jokes, made notes and promised to send a memorandum to Congress. Schoolcraft went to see Senator Thomas, who was friendly but not very encouraging. At a time when oratory was being expended on slavery and free soil, lead mines and natural resources lacked emotional appeal. Thomas sent him to John C. Calhoun, the secretary of war. Calhoun was a dynamic man with a great bush of long dark hair. He was interested in lead because it was used to manufacture bullets but he had no jurisdiction over the mines. The young man's energy in inspecting the lead mines impressed him, however. He had just had a letter from his friend General Lewis Cass, governor of the Michigan Territory. Cass was planning an expedition to look for the sources of the Mississippi. There were said to be potential copper mines on the shores of Lake Superior. Cass wanted a naturalist with a knowledge of mineralogy to accompany the expedition. The job paid a dollar and a half a day.

Schoolcraft had little choice. There was no telling when Congress would get around to action on the lead mines. He was not earning any money and he could not wait indefinitely. And, indeed, his first taste of the wilderness had been an exciting adventure. The expedition was to start immediately. Once more Schoolcraft gave in to the force of circumstances and took another step in the direction of anthropology without knowing it.

In the winter of 1820, snow lay four feet deep in the streets of New York City. Although the ice generally broke up by March, that year the river was frozen solid until April. Schoolcraft took a coach on runners to Albany and westward to Oneida county by the same conveyance. When he reached Buffalo, he took time out to visit the already famous Niagara

Falls. As a geologist, he was fascinated by the way the water was cutting through the layers of rock and gradually moving the falls upstream.

At Buffalo, he boarded the *Walk-in-the-Water*, the first steamship to sail upon Lake Erie. The Indians of the Erie shores were amazed when they first saw her and were responsible for her name. They decided that the spirit of the lake, in return for some favor done him by the white men, had gathered many large fish to draw the ship. She was two years old, had two huge side paddles, a smokestack forward, and since steam was still a sometime uncertain motive power, two square-rigged masts. Her boiler was so large that a quarter of it stuck up in the air. When it was rough she rolled like a whale, one paddlewheel almost out of the water.

Detroit could boast two hundred and fifty houses, some white-painted, some brick, that of General Cass was of cedar logs with board chinking. Cass himself was a large man, square-jawed, with a big nose, big belly and black hair worn long. He explained his plans for the expedition. With the completion of the Erie Canal, immigrants would stream westward. Michigan would become a state. In the meantime, forty thousand Indians had to be dealt with and the area more thoroughly explored and mapped. In trying to reach the source of the Mississippi, the expedition would keep a record of animals, plants, Indian customs and, Schoolcraft in particular, would look for copper and lead.

They were to travel in the thirty-five-foot canoes used by the fur traders. The canoes were strong enough to carry a thousand pounds of fur or provisions and eight men, and were light enough to be carried around rapids by four men. Each canoe carried a small mast and sail, and amidships there was a tent fastened to the gunwales. Anything which might be damaged by water was carefully wrapped in oilskins. The paddlers were French *voyageurs*, woodsmen who had lived in the wilderness so long they had adopted Indian ways. Indeed, many of them were married to Indian women. They wore calico shirts, red woolen caps, breechclouts, deerskin leggings, moccasins and bright red sashes with skin pouches hanging from them.

A crowd gathered to watch the expedition depart. The sky was overcast and a wind came up, with the result that the occupants of the canoe were wet with spray as well as the rain that followed. After a few hours of battling with the rough water they camped. The Ottawa Indians who formed a part of the expedition killed a black bear. When the animal lay still, Schoolcraft was surprised to see one of the Indians shake it by the paw and apparently make a long speech to it. The interpreter explained that they were begging the bear's pardon for killing him, apologizing in particular because a white man had fired one of the bullets. Schoolcraft wanted to know why. He was told that Muck-wa, the bear's spirit, was very powerful and they did not wish to make him angry. This was School-craft's first anthropological observation. Later field workers were to discover that tribes all about the northern regions from North America to Siberia treated the bear with respect and tried to appease its spirit when they killed it.

On the days that followed, Schoolcraft searched for mineral specimens. He found pebbles of jasper, opal, agate, sardonyx and carnelian. When the Indians saw him knocking off bits of rock with his hammer and stowing them in bags, they were amazed. Since rock was not good to eat, was this done for magical purposes, as the Indians saved feathers, fur or animal claws? Schoolcraft had no better explanation and was promptly named in Ottawa Paw-gwa-be-can-e-ga, or "he-who-breaks-rocks."

When the weather was good, the canoes moved along at a

good four miles an hour. One evening when they camped, the Indian leader did a curious thing. He cut a sheet of birch bark, stretched it on the ground and began to draw on it with the sharp point of a knife. When Schoolcraft asked what was going on, he was told they were leaving a message. The artist drew with his knife, first a group of figures with hats on. They were *voyageurs* and soldiers; others without hats were Indians. A man with a sword stood for General Cass. A man with a hammer was, of course, Schoolcraft; the figure with the paper in its hand was Major Douglas, the mapmaker. Three columns of smoke meant they had built three fires. A man with a tongue drawn near his face was the interpreter. A bear and a turtle showed what game they had killed and eight guns what firearms they carried. The bark picture was fastened to a pole with three hatchet cuts in it, which meant they had been travelling for three days. The pole leaned northwest to show the direction in which they were travelling. The figures were crudely drawn, rather like children's pictures, but the interpreter assured Schoolcraft that any Indian seeing them would have no trouble in reading the message. This was, of course, an early kind of picture writing. Schoolcraft recorded it carefully in his diary for it was an Indian custom no one had reported before.

The expedition arrived at Mackinac or, as the Indians called it, Michilimackinac, great turtle. There were two forts and a small French town on a high bluff and many buildings belonging to the American Fur Company, owned by John Jacob Astor, the New York millionaire. Trading schooners were anchored in the harbor where, as the canoes approached, they were greeted with rifle shots. Cass refused to stay long because he wanted to reach the village of Sault Sainte Marie on the river which joined Lake Superior to Lake Huron. Here he planned to hold a council with the Indians and to arrange to leave a garrison of soldiers. Cass was warned that many of the Chippewa at Sault had fought on the side of the British during the War of 1812 and scarcely considered themselves under American jurisdiction. Cass, however, who was called Big Belly by the Indians, was not disturbed.

The town of Sault Sainte Marie got its name from the fact that it was situated on the bank of Saint Mary's River just below a stretch of foaming rapids. The village consisted of about fifteen or twenty houses, log cabins or weathered frame dwellings. The fur company had a store and a boatyard. A few square-riggers were anchored in the river and there was considerable movement of canoes paddled by Indians and fur traders. Near the village loomed the forty domed lodges of the Chippewa encampment.

The leaders of the expedition were entertained by George Johnston, whose father, a fur trader, absent at the time, was married to the daughter of an Indian chief. The mother greeted them shyly but spoke no English and when they sat down to eat, left the table, leaving her daughter Jane to act as hostess. The Johnston house was a comfortable affair, furnished in civilized style and surrounded by a rose garden. It was a house that Schoolcraft was destined to know well. He discovered that Jane had been educated in England and was able to carry on a literary conversation. Meanwhile Cass was learning that the Chippewa were opposed to his plan of leaving a garrison.

The following day, the chiefs filed into a tent which Cass had pitched on the bank of the river. They were dignified and composed but not friendly. Most of them wore calico shirts, breechclouts and red leggings. Around their waists were leather belts from which hung a knife and a pouch. Moccasins were beaded or decorated with dyed porcupine quills. The Chippewa carried lances with chipped stone tips or war clubs.

Over their shoulders were flung capes of blue broadcloth. These last were British woolens, testimony to their relationship with the former enemies of the United States. It was hard for the Americans to forget that the British had been accused of offering a bounty for American scalps.

The chiefs and the white men squatted on the ground. The peace pipe was lit and passed solemnly from hand to hand. Cass understood Indian etiquette and sat silent for five minutes before he began to speak. Pausing now and then for the interpreter to follow his words, he told the chiefs that he came with a message from the president in Washington. The White Father wished to live in peace and friendship with the Chippewa. He wished also to extend his protection and to insure peace between them and their neighbors. In token of his protection he wished to leave some soldiers in the old French fort by the river and perhaps later he would build a new fort. The president had sent some presents to his Indian friends. General Cass hoped they would be pleased with the things he had brought.

Rolls of calico were laid out and pieces of woolen cloth for blankets. There were also knives, silver forks and spoons, tobacco, mirrors, buttons and a few hatchets.

After some consultation, the first reply came from an old chief who said mildly that they hoped to be friends with the president. They had heard both good and bad things about the Americans. They did not see the need for soldiers. When there were soldiers there was always shooting. It might not be easy to prevent the young men from stealing the soldiers' horses. In this way trouble might start. It was better if no soldiers were left in the fort. Then they would believe only good things of the Americans.

Cass tried to answer this diplomatic refusal by saying he would guarantee the soldiers came in peace. They would not be allowed to shoot.

Then suddenly a young chief whom the villagers had named the Count because of his arrogant behavior jumped up. Unlike the others, he was dressed in the red coat with epaulettes of a British officer and wore a British medal pinned to his chest. He brandished his lance and spoke angrily.

They needed no protection, he cried. The Americans were not to be trusted. Only women were afraid of the Foxes or the Sioux. The English redcoats, across the lake, were the friends of the Chippewa and did not speak with double tongues. They did not seek the land of the Chippewa. Soldiers would not be allowed to remain in the fort. The presents given by the redcoats were better than those offered by Cass. Cass should go home and tell the president they did not want them.

He dashed the point of his lance into the ground, kicked the presents aside, and stalked out of the tent, followed slowly by the other chiefs.

In a few moments, the Americans were treated to the sight of a British flag being hoisted above the lodges. Cass, a veteran of the war of 1812, did not take the defiance lying down. He marched straight off to the Count's lodge, pulled up the pole, tore off the offending flag, and trampled on it. The Count, followed by two chiefs, rushed out waving a war club.

Cass paid no attention but treated them to a long harangue in which he said the United States was the greatest nation in the world. It had beaten the redcoats twice. No flag but the Stars and Stripes could be flown in the territory of the United States. Both Indians and whites must obey this regulation. He was not asking permission to put soldiers in the fort. The president had made up his mind and the Indians must obey. If the Count ever raised a foreign flag again, he would be considered a traitor. The soldiers would come against his people and crush them.

He picked up the British flag and walked back to the American encampment. A period of excitement and alarm followed. The fur traders intervened and urged Cass to offer some sort of compromise. He insisted the Indians must come to him. He was the governor of the territory and obliged to take a stand. The power of the United States government would not be respected if he gave in.

Actually, the Americans were in a difficult position. There were seventy or eighty Chippewa in the Indian village, most of them armed, for the British had given them guns. Cass's party numbered sixty-six. He posted a few of them on the outskirts of the village and ordered the townspeople to remain indoors.

The villagers nailed up their windows as the insistent beat of the war drums was heard from the Indian encampment. The next alarming episode was the departure of a number of canoes toward the British shore of the lake. In them the Indians embarked their women and children.

The tension had reached a high point when Mrs. Johnston intervened. She pointed out that the Indians had their own kind of pride. They believed that the earth below and the sky above were theirs. They had never seen American cities and did not understand the power of the white men. She finally suggested that her son should call the chiefs together again and see what he and she could do.

Cass did not forbid this although he sent no official message but instead began melting lead for bullets. Mrs. Johnston and her son worked frantically. They summoned Shingabawossin, the senior chief of the area, to their house. They talked for a long time, explaining the power of the American government. He was convinced. All three went to the Indian encampment. The Count, in full war regalia, his face painted, with a horde of braves behind him, came out to meet them. Shingabawossin ordered him back to the camp for a council. The Count refused. The elder chief told him he was only a little dog without hair. The Count struck at him. Shingabawossin parried the blow, spoke for a long time to the warriors, and finally convinced them. The Count walked off into the woods.

The second parley came off peacefully. It was agreed that four square miles of land which included the site of the village and the old fort were to be ceded to the American government. Both sides relaxed. The pipe of peace went round again.

The whole episode had been an education for Schoolcraft. There was certainly much to be said for the attitude of the Indians as far as their sense of ownership of the land went. Unfortunately, they were an obstacle in the course of the westward movement of the white settlers. From the point of view of American nationalism, Cass had acted firmly. He had made himself respected. From the point of view of objective justice, this was merely one more step in the gradual process of driving the Indians out of their hereditary territory.

Schoolcraft was in some ways a man of his time. He respected and admired Cass and, as yet, he had no close ties with the Indians. He spent considerable time with the Johnston family, however, and especially with Jane. He was later to write a poem in the sentimental style of the period which ended:

> *Adieu smiling circle, wherever I go*
> *In memory still I shall turn to this spot*
> *And cherish thy noble and generous glow,*
> *Till virtue, and friendship, and love be forgot.*

When the expedition finished its work, Schoolcraft returned to Washington to wait for action from Congress on the lead mines. He also worked on a book, using the material from his diary. He soon received a new invitation from Cass to join a second expedition to gather information concerning the resources of the Mississippi Valley. Cass was determined that the eastern public should know more about the Middle West. With still no alternative in sight, Schoolcraft was glad to accept. On July 3, 1821, the expedition set out from Detroit in a large canoe with a mast and sail and an awning with side curtains which acted as a sort of cabin.

At Fort Wayne, Schoolcraft visited a school for Indian children. A bored teacher wrote the letters of the alphabet upon a primitive blackboard and forced the children to repeat them in chorus. Schoolcraft stared at the dirty brown faces of the children. In some cases, their eyes were red and inflamed from a painful disease, called trachoma. They mumbled the letters halfheartedly or sat in silence. When they were dismissed, they fled out of the door into the woods. The teacher, a seedy Baptist clergyman, considered them stupid and unteachable. When Schoolcraft asked questions, he discovered scarcely any of them knew English. The alphabet was therefore totally meaningless.

By this time Schoolcraft was pondering over the Indian problem. If the white settlers took their land away, the American government certainly owed them something. But such perfunctory and pointless pretense at education was certainly not the answer. Whenever they encountered Indian bands, the braves begged General Cass for whiskey, which he refused to give them. Schoolcraft was soon to see the effect of this contribution of the white man's civilization.

On the Maumee River, he spent the night in an Indian dwelling. The settlement was located in an oak grove beyond which were prairies on which the horses grazed, bells hung from their necks in case they strayed. Some of the Indians owned cows, hogs and poultry and raised corn, pumpkins and beans. As Cass and Schoolcraft sat in the lodge, they could see figures moving around a large fire. Then shouts and raised voices were heard. As time passed, the noise grew louder, quarrels broke out. There were screams of hysterical laughter. By midnight they were singing, shouting, crying at the same time. At this point, an old squaw lighted a candle and began taking down all the knives which were hung on the walls. She bundled them into her blanket and carried them away. Cass shook his head. From somewhere they had gotten whiskey and this was the result. The Maumees were making the change to agriculture which was in their favor, but through trade with the white men they obtained whiskey, which they were unable to use in moderation.

There was one other brush with the Indians. A group of hunters demanded whiskey, which was refused. A little later, when the canoes were rounding a bend in the river, the hunters leaped from the bank and overturned one. When Cass had the presence of mind to cry out "Don't fire!," the attackers vanished. Eventually the wet provisions were salvaged and order was restored. The only loss was a keg of whiskey which had been carried off in the confusion.

Schoolcraft could see that few scientific efforts had been made to learn something about the native way of life. General Cass was collecting material for a book on Indian lore, but Indian languages were not even classified. These were challenging problems but Schoolcraft was a mineralogist and a geologist. There was work to do in his own field. The primary and secondary rocks of the continent were not even mapped.

Beyond New Harmony, Schoolcraft visited some lead mines, still thinking of such improvements as installing steam engines to haul up ore. When the party reached the Illinois River, they began to traverse open plains where the immense herds of buffalo pastured. Here Schoolcraft visited a Fox Indian village. He moved among tall skin tepees with bright designs painted on them and wondered if these markings were related to the picture writing he had discovered among the Ottawa. The open flaps of the tents revealed glimpses of native family life. In his journal he described a little scene with a good deal of feeling: "A Fox Indian, sitting in his tent, held in his arms his infant son who, as usual at this season, when not bound in the cradle, was perfectly naked. With a fan of feathers he drove away the mosquitos and flies from the infant's body, frequently suspending this watchful labor to press the child to his lips; and evincing by his countenance a tender care mixed with high gratification. . . ." In a few lines he makes clear that the Indians were becoming people to him. He was too sensitive and too observant a man not to feel some sympathy for them. He was an exception in a period in which most Americans believed the only good Indian was a dead Indian.

The party finally reached Chicago where Cass was to meet with a group of tribes and to use his diplomatic skills in convincing them they must cede more land to the whites. Chicago in 1821 consisted of a stockaded fort with a few cannons and a scattering of shabby wooden buildings built by traders. On one side were spread the blue waters of the lake, and on the other plains covered with prairie grass and buffalo chips. It was now summer and a forest of Indian tepees arose on the prairie. Dogs barked, children ran about, and the earth resounded with the drumbeat of horses' hooves as young braves galloped and wheeled about the encampment. They jingled with silver ornaments, their bodies gay with black, red, yellow and white paint, their hair shining with grease, waving lances tipped with feathers and holding small round shields. They managed horses with much showmanship to impress rival warriors and to arouse the admiration of the young women. These young warriors were always a source of danger, for according to the Indian code, advancement in life consisted in counting coup, that is touching, wounding, or killing an enemy in battle. In consequence, they were always impatient, anxious for war rather than peace and sometimes at odds with the cautious policies of the older chiefs.

The chiefs assembled, splendidly dressed, ceremonial paint on their faces and bodies, earrings in their ears, and war bonnets on their heads. They represented about three thousand Ottawa, Pottawatamies and Chippewa. Cass was empowered to buy from them some five million acres of land, an area which is today northern Illinois, Indiana and western Michigan. After each speech, the Indians said "Hau!" solemnly in chorus, equivalent to "We hear."

Cass argued that game was scarce in the territory in question and that he would pay well for the land. He also told the Indians not to drink whiskey but to remain clear-headed for their deliberations. The chiefs replied they had heard and would retire for consultation.

Some of the speeches made the following day are indeed moving as these dignified orators fought against the sophistication and power of the white man. One of them ended, "You are never satisfied. I am an Indian, a redskin, and I live by hunting and fishing, but my country is already too small and I do not know how to bring up my children if I give it all away. Indeed, we have hardly enough to cover the bones of our tribe. Do not think we have a bad opinion of you. We speak to you with good hearts and the feelings of a friend. We all shake hands with you. Behold our warriors, our women, our children. Take pity on us and our words." He argued that the land was given them by "The Master of Life," but Cass tirelessly and shrewdly argued that they were thinly spread and their cornfields occupied no more space than the flies on the surface of the table in front of him. The Indians pleaded, stubbornly held back, but Cass wore them down. After some days, the natives gave in, signed a treaty, and, for a few thousand dollars, an area comprising more than two states came under the control of the United States. Cass could argue that he offered the best bargain he could and it was better than driving the Indians off by force as many military men would have liked to do.

Schoolcraft was attacked by a stomach complaint at the treaty conference and did not return to the East until December of 1821. He published several papers on geological subjects and worked on his report on the copper mines for Secretary Calhoun. His fame as a natural scientist was growing. Ex-presidents James Madison and John Adams wrote letters congratulating him on his articles. His old teacher, Professor Hall of Middlebury, wrote a letter in support of his candidacy for director of the government mines, saying, "It seems according to your account that these mines are an exhaustless source of wealth to the United States. I should feel glad to have them put under your superintendence and to have you nurture up a race of expert mineralogists. . . ." He was granted more interviews with President Monroe and Secretary Calhoun, but Congress still did not act. Schoolcraft published his journal of the first trip with Cass, which was well received. Finally he was faced with another important decision.

Congress was about to pass a bill, creating a separate Indian agency in Florida. At the same time Calhoun planned to transfer the western agency to Sault Sainte Marie and also build a new fort and garrison it. Cass was also in favor of the plan. Senator Thomas offered to confirm the president's nomination of Schoolcraft as Indian agent. All Schoolcraft's friends were working together, it seemed, and it would have been ungrateful to reject their help. On the other hand, he considered himself a mineralogist, not an expert on Indians. It was almost comic the way forces over which he had no control pushed him gradually in a direction he had never planned to go. But it was, after all, only a temporary decision.

On July 6, 1822, Schoolcraft disembarked from the steamer *Superior* along with Colonel Brady, the head of the new garrison. A crowd of Indians and settlers greeted them. Presently the troops were landed, the American flag was raised and the band played as it marched by. It was the first time that American authority had been implemented by a permanent garrison since the area had been taken over from the French by the treaty of 1783. For the first time Schoolcraft met the trader Johnston, whose wife and children had been so hospitable on his first visit.

Schoolcraft's task was to see that the previous year's treaty ceding the land was carried out, to keep the Indians from intriguing with the authorities in Canada, to cement relations with the Chippewa, and to carry out a certain amount of what we would call social service.

At his first conference with the Indians, Brady formed his men into a hollow square in front of the tent in which the chiefs assembled. Schoolcraft made a speech through his Irish interpreter and was answered majestically by Shingabawossin. The Count, whose name was Sassaba, still in his British uniform, created a disturbance and walked out. His brother had been killed by the American forces during the war of 1812, which partially accounted for his hostility. Presents were distributed and all went well.

Schoolcraft dined with the Johnstons and presently he was invited to live with them. He was told the story of Johnston's marriage to Woman-of-the-Green-Valley. When her father, an important chief, agreed to the marriage, she fasted and stayed in a spirit lodge until she dreamed of a white man who came to her with a cup in his hand. He said to her, "Poor thing, why do you punish yourself? Why do you fast? Here is food for you." This, she believed, was her guardian spirit and meant she must marry the white man. But she was so frightened, thinking Johnston to be some sort of spirit or a god, that after her marriage she remained rolled up in a blanket in a corner for weeks and would not let him touch her until her father intervened. She still never sat down to the table with her husband and it was explained to Schoolcraft that the Indians believed that although women were weaker than men, a dangerous magic clung to them. Men must be careful not to become affected by this magic which would destroy their skill in hunting and their bravery in war. For this reason, curious tabus were carefully obeyed.

Meanwhile Schoolcraft had set up his office in a fourteen by twelve log cabin heated by a big iron stove. In front of the agency a green meadow was covered with lodges and swept down to the river, here three quarters of a mile wide. From his window he could look out on his people. The livestock, their family life, their games and ceremonies were spread before him. Believing that communication was of first importance, he concerned himself with their language. His interpreter knew enough Chippewa to obtain meat and drink, to buy and sell and not much else even though he was married to an Indian wife. Schoolcraft set about compiling a grammar.

Schoolcraft's thoughtful habit of getting to the bottom of things both resulted in better relations with the Indians and also began to provide him with much new information concerning their customs which he carefully recorded in his journals.

He soon had to settle a conflict between the Indians and the soldiers. The latter were cutting a road up a hill to a spot where they planned to cut wood for a stockade. The Indians complained that the soldiers had cut shoots from what seemed to be a partially decayed stump. It was part of a huge hollow mountain ash which made a sound when the wind blew through it. It was considered the residence of a spirit because it sounded like the noise made by a magician's drum. Offerings of twigs were laid at its foot by the hunters. Schoolcraft, unable to prevent the soldiers from clearing the ground, made a present of tobacco to the Indians which they could use as an offering.

Again, he had to intervene when a thin peeled sapling with bits of scarlet and blue cloth and beads tied to the top was taken by a soldier from in front of one of the Indian lodges and used for a tent pole. He discovered that it was an offering to the spirits to drive away sickness which had attacked one of the inmates of the lodge. In this case, he insisted that the pole be given back.

One day, an Indian named White Bird with a silver medal around his neck appeared. It had been given to him by General Cass when he had acted as a guide on their first expedition. White Bird looked haggard and melancholy. He explained that he was an outcast. Evil medicine had been made against him because he had shown the white man copper, the source of the Indian's wealth. The Master of Life was angry with him. A few weeks later, the young man became quite ill. The army doctor visited him but could not find any physical ailment. Medicines were given to him but he continued to pine away with what Schoolcraft called "some secret mental canker." "He died because he *would die*," the doctor said. This was perhaps the first recorded case of a preliterate dying for psychological reasons because of his belief in harmful magic. Schoolcraft's intimacy with the Johnston family resulted in all sorts of discoveries, the most important being that of Chippewa mythology. Familiar as he was with Greek and Roman myths, it came as a revelation that these people, who had generally been looked upon as savages, had created a wealth of stories concerning their traditional heroes and many tales explaining events and happenings in the natural world around them.

For instance, there was the legend of the white fish. In the old days, a well-known chief was living some distance from Saint Mary's. He had a wife and two sons. His was not a good woman. A neighboring hunter used to visit her while the chief was away. The sons became angry and told their father. The chief, to avenge his honor, killed his wife with his war club, buried her under the ashes of his campfire and moved the lodge to another place. But the spirit of the woman never left him in peace. It appeared to the father and sons in dreams. They used to wake up trembling with fright. Finally they decided to leave that part of the country. In their travels they came to Saint Mary's falls. Suddenly, to their horror, they saw a skull rolling along the beach. They knew at once whose skull it was and they trembled with fright. Then they saw a huge old crane sitting on a rock in the midst of the rapids. They called out, "Grandfather Crane, we are persecuted by a spirit. Come and take us across the falls so that we may escape her." The crane flew to them and said, "Do not touch the back of my head. There is a sore spot. If you touch it, I shall have to throw you into the rapids." One by one he took the three men across the river. Then the skull cried out, "Grandfather Crane, carry me over, too. I have lost my children and I am sad." The crane said to the skull, "Do not touch my head. There is a sore spot. If you touch it, I shall have to throw you into the rapids." The crane picked up the skull but it could not restrain its curiosity and touched the back of the bird's head. The crane threw the skull into the rapids where it floated, bouncing from rock to rock, until it was battered to pieces. The brain fell out of its bony case into the water and immediately took the form of a new fish, whitish in color. Ever since that time, the waters at the foot of the falls have been full of whitefish. The brothers became the ancestors of the Chippewa tribe and the chiefs at Saint Mary's called the crane their *dodaim*. Dodaim, called by some explorers "totem," was the name for an animal consid-

ered to be a badge or crest of a grouping within a tribe called
a clan. This was an institution which was to give rise to decades
of study as the science of anthropology developed.

Schoolcraft was present at the funeral of an Indian called
Strong Sky. The man had been killed in a drunken brawl with
a half-breed. The killer had gotten away and, since neither one
was white, no great effort was made to find the murderer. The
Indian agent had to accept this as the code of the frontier.
The man was laid out by his relatives, dressed in his best, a
turban of blue cloth wound about his head.

At the funeral, the dead man was wrapped in a blanket and
laid in a coffin beside the grave. An aged "speaker," as Indian
orators were called, stepped from the little group of Chippewa
and addressed the dead man. He mentioned his good qualities:
he had provided meat for his family, he had always spoken
the truth. Now he had reached the end of his journey but his
friends and relatives would one day follow him to the land
of the dead where they would all meet again. This journey
would be difficult and he would be beset by many evil spirits.
His friends, however, would make strong magic to help him.
Now, for the last time he said goodby.

When the speaker finished, Strong Sky's brother stepped
forward, removed the turban, and cut a lock of hair to remember him by. The headdress was replaced, the coffin closed and
placed in the grave. Two strong poles were laid across the
open grave. The brother went to the widow and stood beside
her. The speaker talked to them both. He urged the brother
to do his duty. He must hunt well and bring back enough meat
and fish for his sister now that she had no man to care for her.
He must regard her children as his own. He then took the
widow by the hand and led her across the grave over the two
poles. That night a small flickering fire was built at the head
of the grave.

After talking with Strong Sky's squaw, Schoolcraft learned that the murderer was a trader who bartered whiskey for furs. The episode was one more example of the evils resulting from the sale of liquor to the Indians. Schoolcraft had to face the problem of liquor continually. He never touched it himself and he could not help being annoyed when Indians traded all their game and furs for whiskey and then, when destitute, came to beg from the agency. Once a drunken Indian called him father and asked the agent to look upon him as a child. Schoolcraft told him firmly he would be glad to but that reasonable children did not trouble their fathers too often or beg for things they did not need.

Congress had passed a law prohibiting the importation of liquor into the territory but nothing was done about enforcing it. According to the fur traders' philosophy the Indians were lazy and whiskey was the only reward which would bring in the furs. Moreover they said they had to compete with the Canadians who were restrained by no law. If Schoolcraft threatened to withhold license to trade, he was told they could make trouble for him in Washington. Schoolcraft had to learn to live with John Jacob Astor's American Fur Company, but he resolved to do what he could with his pen to make his fellow Americans aware of the situation of the Indians.

One tragedy he was powerless to avert. Sassaba, the Count, continued to brood and drink heavily. He had been treated as an officer by the British and insisted that the Americans were unjustly claiming British territory. He once appeared at a meeting, at which food was being distributed, drunk and naked except for a grey wolfskin tied about his neck. He began to shout curses and make obscene gestures until he was led away.

A few weeks later, after a prolonged drinking bout at a village above the falls, he decided to shoot the rapids. While standing up to hoist a blanket to the mast, he capsized the

canoe into the swiftest part of the current. His friend managed
to swim ashore but Sassaba was never seen again. Schoolcraft
wrote his epitaph:

> *The Falls were thy grave, as they leapt mad along,*
> *And the roar of the waters thy funeral song:*
> *So wildly, so madly thy people for aye,*
> *Are rapidly, ceaselessly passing away.*

He visited the chief's tent after his death. It contained a set
of silver teaspoons and tablespoons, knives, forks, cups and
saucers. His officer's coat, sword and epaulettes hung from one
of the poles. In a chest lay some ruffled linen shirts, a pair of
gloves, shoes and stockings and an umbrella, none of which
he had ever used but which he proudly displayed to visitors.

The long winter evenings at Sault, when no mail arrived
and the snow piled up until the inhabitants had to dig like
woodchucks to get from one house or one lodge to another,
when the only means of journeying on the surface of the drifts
was a pair of snowshoes, when the temperature went down to
twenty-five below zero, Schoolcraft worked on his Chippewa
grammar. He had written to General Cass concerning his discovery of an Indian mythology and his mentor had written
back enthusiastically urging him to investigate the subject.
About the same time, the spring of 1823, when horse-drawn
vehicles were able to reach Sault Sainte Marie from Detroit
by traversing the ice, a letter came from a friend in Washington which put an end to his earlier hopes. The plan for the
establishment of a Superintendent of Mines had been dropped
and instead the government had decided to sell its Missouri
mines to private owners. Schoolcraft was not too deeply disappointed. He felt at home in Sault. As soon as an addition
to the Johnston's house could be built, he planned to marry
Jane. His interest in Indian study was taking up more and

more of his time. He wrote in his diary, "It is probable that my destiny is now fixed." And indeed it was for, although the term was not yet in use, he had once and for all become an anthropologist.

That summer, he and Jane were married. It was a daring step for an educated, middle-class American. Indians were generally looked down upon as an inferior race. They were not yet considered to be romantic figures. It was true that the French writer Jean-Jacques Rousseau had suggested that the primitive in a state of nature was happier than the prisoner of an unjust and artificial society, but that did not mean that you married one. Schoolcraft tells us nothing of his feelings or the struggles he may have gone through to make this decision. We do know that his mother wrote she was troubled by his marriage and could not understand it. His mother, however, was very far away. Jane and he were near enough of an age and drawn together by their shared interest in the customs of her mother's people.

The years that followed were busy ones. Schoolcraft had his daily office hours during which the Indians visited him like relief clients, begging for provisions and tools. It was his task to decide whether they were British sympathizers and hence undeserving of American relief. To one of these ambiguous characters he pointed out that, since he had been receiving presents from the British Father in summer, he should now go back and apply to him for help in winter.

Toward the end of the year 1824, a trader brought back a story of an Indian massacre. A war party of Chippewa on a raid against the Sioux happened upon a trader and murdered and scalped him. The scalp was sent to Schoolcraft in a small black coffin by the head chief of the region who disclaimed any connection with the killing and asked what should be done. The scalp with a full report was sent to Washington.

Meanwhile Schoolcraft and his new wife made a trip east during which Jane had a success as the northern Pocohontas. Schoolcraft reaffirmed his friendship with Calhoun, now vice-president under John Quincy Adams. He saw his *Narrative of Travels in the Mississippi Valley* printed, and returned to Sault just in time to receive a delegation of Chippewa who had come to the agency to surrender the murderers of Finley, the American trader. The whole tribe had been threatened with military retaliation and had decided to abide by the white man's law. Schoolcraft examined the murderers, made a severe speech censoring them, marched them around, guarded by troops with fixed bayonets, and let them go. He then hung a silver medal around the neck of the chief who surrendered them. He felt he had followed Cass's rule—perfect justice, no yielding, no trickery.

The following day, he set out to meet Cass at Prairie du Chien in the Mississippi Valley where he was to meet a great convocation of chiefs. With his retinue of local chiefs, a flag flying at the bow of his canoe, he felt quite like a visiting potentate. Cass met him with open arms. The usual splendid array of warriors in feathers and paint, necklaces of grizzly bears' teeth, headdresses of red horsehair tied to a scalp lock like a Roman helmet, were moving about the banks, beating drums and shaking lances. There were Ottawa, Pottawatomie, Iowa Sacs, Foxes, Dakota and Winnebago. Cass had had the statesmanlike idea of assembling the Algonquin and Sioux tribes and trying to draw a clearly defined boundary between them, thus hoping to put a stop to the continual hostilities. He wished, in this way, to avoid such episodes as the murder of the trader, Finley.

Negotiations went on for a whole month as commissioners and agents went from group to group, studying Indian bark maps and picture writing. Eventually a line of demarcation

was worked out. The chiefs made enthusiastic speeches but
actually the whole undertaking was in opposition to the horse
culture of the Plains Indians whose vitality depended on raids,
counting coup and military success.

On the way home, Schoolcraft was obliged to camp on a
stony block on the shore of Lake Huron to wait out a terrible
equinoctial storm, beating down with gales of wind. Shivering
in his tent for two days, he fell into a depressed mood and
wrote one of his best poems:

> What narrowed pleasures swell the bosom here,
> A shore most sterile and a clime severe,
> Where every shrub seems stunted in its size,
> Where genius sickens and where fancy dies.
> If to the shore I cast my anxious eye,
> There broken rocks and sand comingled lie,
> Mixed with the wreck of shells and weeds and wood,
> Crushed by the storm and driven by the flood.

The third day, on which they set off again, turned out to be
one of the worst in his life. The sail was reefed to less than
four feet but the wind ripped at it until it looked as though
it would not hold. The big canoe was flung up and down like
a chip and water poured over the gunwale with every gust.
The helmsman tried desperately to head into the waves, mut-
tering prayers to the saints. There seemed no end to the
struggle. Chilled to the bone, their joints stiff, their lips blue,
they battled on and on. At last they got into the lee of a small
island and from there into the straits and home at last. When
Jane ran to meet him, he could not tell her exactly what had
happened but deep within him there was a sense of his own
littleness and the vast indifference of the universe which he
would carry with him all of his life.

Schoolcraft continued his struggle with the fur company

over whiskey and appointed his brother-in-law, George, to a subagency on Lake Superior where he could watch over the activities of the traders. In 1832, after more incidents between the Chippewa and the Sioux and a whirlwind trip of pacification made by Schoolcraft, a new and most important expedition was organized, whose aims were to curb hostilities, investigate the fur trade, obtain statistics concerning the number of Indians in the Minnesota region and to vaccinate them against smallpox.

Since Cass was now secretary of war, Schoolcraft had his tacit backing for a project both had had in mind for some time. This was the discovery of the source of the Mississippi. In 1805, Lieutenant Zebulon Pike had gotten as far as Red Cedar Lake. Cass, in 1820, had reached a lake farther north which was now named Cass Lake. The real source, however, was farther north somewhere in the unexplored territory which is now Minnesota. Nothing was said about the Mississippi project officially, but Schoolcraft made careful plans. His brother-in-law, George, now thirty-eight, who spoke both French and Chippewa, acted as interpreter and was in charge of supplies. Among the experts who went along was the doctor, Douglas Houston, already at twenty-two a professor at Rensselaer Polytechnic, a botanist as well as a mineralogist. A young lieutenant in his twenties, a mapmaker, was in charge of the troops. Finally, in order to investigate the possibility of mission schools, Schoolcraft took with him the Reverend William Boutwell from Michilimackinac. All told, with the soldiers, Chippewa and French paddlers, the party numbered about thirty. Cass had managed to pry $3,000 out of the War Department for expenses, and aside from provisions, the expedition took along $700 worth of presents for the Indians.

The party started on June 7, in several canoes and boats with flags flying. The soldiers never became good paddlers

and their boats generally lagged behind. The doctor was busy
with natural science, for Schoolcraft had now given up this
study and devoted himself to Indian customs. The Reverend
Boutwell, who had never gone exploring before, was distinctly
unhappy most of the time. He emerges as a comic figure. From
the beginning he insisted that no travelling should be done
on Sunday.

When Sunday came, he requested the services of George
Johnston and assembled the Indians and French paddlers in
front of the tents. The missionary ordered the interpreter to
read passages from the Bible and finally a tract, "Two Ways
of Life," in French. The *voyageurs* grinned and whispered; the
Indians sat expressionless. As soon as the meeting was over,
the Frenchmen produced a pack of cards and began to gamble,
shouting and swearing loudly. Boutwell was scandalized. He
retired to arm his spirit by reading *Pilgrim's Progress*.

When the party encamped on the St. Louis River, rifle shots
brought him flying out of his tent, sure they were being attacked. Instead, a band of thirty Indians from the interior
came dancing by with a hop step to the beating of drums.
Their leader had two foxtails pointed forward like horns
mounted on his head. Poor Boutwell had visions of the devil.

By next Sunday, Schoolcraft was again confronted by
Boutwell. From nearby the squeak of fiddles proved that the
*voyageurs* were amusing themselves by dancing. Boutwell
admitted he was defeated by the French idolators but now he
heard the Indians were to have a dance. Schoolcraft tried to
explain that native dancing had a religious significance. Boutwell raged against superstition. Schoolcraft forbade the dance
but, all during the day, the chiefs came to him to inquire if
Sunday was over.

At a meeting with a chief by the name of Mozojeed near
Sandy Lake, Boutwell told him that some one would be sent

to him to teach his children about God and Heaven, if he wished it. The chief looked confused and replied through the interpreter, "Tell the white jossakeed (magician) I have no children."

The expedition reached the Savanna River on its way to Leech Lake and here encountered one of the most difficult portages of the journey. Ordinarily a portage meant carrying the canoes and goods over dry land around a part of the river which was too shallow or too dangerous to be navigated. Here, however, the high water had spilled out over acres of ground, creating large areas of soft mud which was thin enough to float a canoe loaded with baggage. The men had to disembark and push the canoes, wading through mud that reached to the knees or, at times, to the waist. Sometimes it gave place to grass and reeds thinly covered with water. Under these conditions, the party struggled on for three days. Even Lieutenant Allen, young and strong as he was, longed for it to be over. Boutwell panted on, bleeding profusely from mosquito bites, his face smeared with mud. The rest of the men staggered in an uneven line, shoving and hauling the canoes. Some of the *voyageurs* had lost a trouser leg, their shirts were in rags and, since their moccasins were worn through, their toes were bruised and raw. Schoolcraft, who was used to every sort of travel, plunged on ahead tirelessly.

At Cass Lake the expedition picked up a skilled guide, named Yellow Head, who said he could take them to the headwaters of the river. Here a scalp dance was in progress. One of the band had been killed in battle with the Sioux and the ceremony was a part of the funeral rites. The dead brave's body had been placed on a platform of slats raised high in the air on four poles. The grass around these graves was worn in paths from continual dancing. The widow looked on while a large group of squaws danced in a circle. The new scalp and two old ones were suspended by thongs from hoops with five foot handles. The long hair of the scalps was decorated with feathers and allowed to hang down. Three young squaws waved the scalps, shouted and sang as they danced, their skins dripping with perspiration. The assembled onlookers, men, women and children, sang, beat drums and shook rattles. Every now and then the dancers paused while one of the leaders made a speech exalting the victory over the Sioux. Presents for the widow were thrown into the center of the circle. To the whites the ceremony was monotonous and repetitious, but the Indians kept it up till late that night.

The next leg of the journey Schoolcraft carried out with only five light canoes. After a portage through sandy plains and easy paddling through two lakes and a small river, they encountered a series of rapids full of large boulders. They struggled through ten portages. Next, they entered a handsome lake with wooded shores; beyond it a river split in two, following Yellow Head, they entered the left branch.

That night, they camped on the low marshy shores of a small lake, thinly wooded with evergreens. A steamy rain fell and dampened the spirits of the party. It seemed that they were engaged in a wild goose chase. Schoolcraft, however, would not think of giving up. The next day was clear. With aching muscles they faced more portages and more mosquitos as the channel shrank to a mere brook, edged with wild rice, and its surface dotted with yellow pond lilies. They reached the last portage. Everything had to be carried. Schoolcraft describes it as follows:

I charged myself with a spyglass and portfolio. Dr. Houghton carried a plant press. Each one had something and the men toiled with five canoes, beds, tent, etc. The path was one of the most intricate and tangled I ever knew. Tornados appeared to have cast down trees in every direction. A soft spongy moss that gave way under the tread covered the interstices between the fallen timber. The toil and fatigue was incessant. At length we ascended the first height. It was an arid eminence of pebble and erratic blocks bearing small gray pines and shrubbery. This constituted our first pause. On descending it, we were again plunged among brambles. Path there was none, or trail that any mortal eye but an Indian's could trace. We ascended another eminence. We descended it and entered a thicket of bramble, every twig of which seemed placed to bear some token of our wardrobe as we passed. To avoid this the guides passed through a lengthened shallow pond beyond which walking was easier. Hill succeeded hill. It was a hot July day and the sun shone brightly. Although we were evidently passing an alpine height where a long winter reigned and the vegetation bore every indication of being imperfectly developed . . . moss hung abundantly from the trees. . . . At length a glitter of water appeared.

The leaders of the group ran down the hill and came out upon a clear, green body of water. The end of the lake could be clearly seen surrounded by hills, there was no stream larger than a brook running into it. Here was the end of the trail, the source of the greatest river in America. Schoolcraft was the first man to have traversed it from mouth to source, a distance of 3,160 miles.

In the middle of the lake there was a beautiful island; near its shore a deer stood knee deep in the water. Far off the shrill cries of loons could be heard. The sun rippled on the water. The rest of the party came running up. They shook hands and slapped each other on the back. After raising the American flag and firing a salute, they decided to name the island after Schoolcraft. The lake he christened Itaska, a garbled combination of the words for head and truth in Latin.

When the party reached Leech Lake on the trip back,

Schoolcraft had a conference with Flat Mouth, a leading Chippewa chief who had led the recent attack upon the Sioux. He was a well-known speaker and a man of such authority that he had actually ordered a fur trader under house arrest when the white man displeased him.

It was Schoolcraft's task to do what he could toward influencing this Indian leader in the direction of peace. While Dr. Houghton vaccinated stoical warriors, brave small boys and screaming girls, Schoolcraft had a solemn conference with Flat Mouth, who was already disillusioned with the great boundary meeting which had supposedly settled the hostilities between the Algonquin and the Sioux. He maintained that the United States government had not punished the aggression of the Sioux, during which his own son had been killed along with fifty other members of his band. In a dramatic gesture he flung down medals, flags and wampum, given him by the government, all stained with red paint and cried, "You see how it is. The blood of these men covers everything. I want you to wash these things clean. I have taken scalps but not enough to avenge the death of my people. They are poor and defenseless, they are so poor the trees weep for them. If I do not receive help from the United States, I will go to the British."

Schoolcraft was in a difficult position. The United States government was in no position to police the long and vaguely defined boundary between the two peoples. Although Cass's efforts had been well-meaning, they were unrealistic since they went against the military culture of the Indians. All Schoolcraft could do was to urge Flat Mouth not to attack, to do no more than defend his people. At the end of the meeting, the chief asked for a white shirt which was given to him. It was a curious request but when the time came for the party to leave, the chief appeared on the shore wearing shoes, stockings, pantaloons, a blue army coat, the frilled white shirt, a hat, and even a pair of gloves. He had delivered his speech in defense of his people in Indian dress but now, with the Indian sense of ceremonial attire, had put on the white man's costume as a gesture of respect for the American government.

In 1832, Schoolcraft moved to a large consolidated agency at Michilimackinac where he worked on his book of Algonquin mythology. Four years later he went to Washington to undertake his last important negotiation with the native tribes. As American civilization rolled westward, the pressure to acquire more land increased. He was asked to deal with the Indians once more. Schoolcraft had at one time figured out that a single hunter, to keep his family supplied with food, required some fifty thousand acres. Such areas were no longer available. Game had already begun to fail in the lower Michigan peninsula. The Indians, more and more dependent upon civilized goods, were deeply in debt to the traders. They were no longer proud and independent, instead they actually sent a delegation to Washington to peddle the only asset they owned, what was left of their land. Since Schoolcraft had been appointed special commissioner by President Jackson, he found out that those in Washington represented only a small number of the bands involved. He immediately invited delegates from all of the Chippewa and Ottawa groups throughout the territory. During the council, held in Washington, he obtained sixteen million acres at twelve and a half cents an acre, in comparison with other land deals of the period a fairly liberal settlement. Indeed, in 1867, Russia got only two cents an acre for Alaska.

Schoolcraft tried with each of his treaties to arrange for instruction in agriculture so that the Indians might have a new means of subsistence. He believed, too, that free boarding schools which educated a few individual children far from their own people were worse than useless. "Children who are drawn away to foreign boarding schools become estranged from their tribes, and when they return it is too often found that they have acquired a species of knowledge which places them so far above their people that they become objects of distrust." He felt that local schools to which the Indians could contribute were the answer. It took a hundred years before this sensible policy was adopted by the United States Office of Indian Affairs.

During the years at Michilimackinac, Schoolcraft was visited by famous traveling authors, elected to various learned societies, and continued to publish accounts of his travels. His journal recounting the discovery of Lake Itaska came out in 1834 but it was not until 1839 that his important and truly anthropological book, *Algic Researches* was published in two volumes. This was a collection of all the Chippewa mythology he had gleaned from his years on the frontier. Some had been dictated by Mrs. Johnston, some he had extracted from chiefs who visited the agency, some had been obtained for him by George Johnston. All along Jane had worked faithfully, explaining, translating, clarifying the heritage of her mother's people. It was the first collection of preliterate mythology ever gathered in the field. Such oral storytelling among hunting and fishing peoples tends to be repetitious and to include episodes which polite literature of the time considered indecent. Schoolcraft removed such episodes, cut the repetitions and to some extent weakened the style with his own period sense of literary decorum. The material, however, was valuable, particularly since it revealed a cycle of tales dealing with the culture hero, Manbozho, and also such themes as the destruction of the world by a flood which were to be found in other oral literatures.

Schoolcraft himself stated the real importance of the collection of tales. "Their chief value I have ever thought to consider is the insight they give into the dark cave of the Indian mind—its beliefs, dogmas, opinions—its secret modes of turning over its thought—its real philosophy; and it is for this trait that I believe posterity will sustain this book." He was indeed correct for it constituted a beginning in the study of preliterate psychology. Years later, on Dec. 14, 1855, he received an interesting letter:

> Dear Sir,
> I send you by mail a copy of *The Song of Hiawatha*, a poem founded upon Indian legends, which I beg you to accept as a token of my great regard and an acknowledgment of my obligations to you; for without your books I could not have written mine.
> If you have time to look over *Hiawatha*, you will find that I have adhered to the old myths and you will be amazed to hear that a critic in *The National Intelligencer* accuses me of drawing many of these legends from the Finnish poem, *Kalevala.* Any suggestions from you I shall value highly.
> > Yours faithfully,
> > HENRY LONGFELLOW

Since Longfellow was the most famous poet of his time, Schoolcraft was pleased and flattered that he had furnished him with material. Longfellow, of course, diluted the oral tales still more with his own style and by handling them in terms of an alien epic meter. Schoolcraft, with his usual desire for accuracy, wrote to *The National Intelligencer* that Longfellow took only the *Kalevala* meter. The legends were Indian: "In making the collection the narrators were often my guests and the matter was written down with all its interlocutions on the spot."

In 1842, the Democrats were beaten by the Whig "log cabin and cider campaign," which swept Harrison and Tyler into the White House. Schoolcraft's supporters had been Whigs. His fight with the fur traders over the whiskey issue had made him enemies. After nineteen years as a government servant, he was dismissed on the charge, never substantiated, that he had used his official influence improperly. He denied and fought the charge unsuccessfully. He was probably a victim of political patronage.

By this time Jane had been ill for some time and was dragging out a miserable existence addicted to sedatives. Their two children, John and Janee, were at school in the East. Schoolcraft left the scene of his adventures and triumphs sadly. The rest of his life, although he was to continue his work, was to be full of sadness and suffering.

That same year Jane died suddenly while he was on a trip to Europe. Schoolcraft lived in New York for a time with his two children, Janee, blonde, pretty, taking after her father, and John, handsome, dark-skinned and destined to cause his father nothing but anxiety.

Schoolcraft lectured, started an anthropological review, and eventually was hired by New York State to take a census of the Iroquois Indians. While he was traveling about the state, he was invited by a young lawyer, Lewis Morgan, to address the first public meeting of a society he had created, the New Confederation of the Iroquois. Morgan had invited Schoolcraft to join his organization and wanted him to appear in Indian costume. Morgan had become involved in a study of the Iroquois through his friendship with the son of a Seneca chief, Ely Parker. Morgan was to become the second famous American anthropologist. At this period, he was a naïve student but there is no doubt that the older man's work lent impetus to his studies. The picture of the rather staid Schoolcraft standing patiently in a feather headdress while members of Morgan's club marched around him waving bows and arrows and singing a war song in their initiation ceremony is an amusing one.

In 1846, Schoolcraft married Mary Howard, a southern

woman with strong proslavery convictions. Younger than he, she had intellectual pretensions; after his death, she wrote an autobiographical novel in which she thinly disguised the events of her life with Schoolcraft. At the time Schoolcraft married he presented his "Plan for the Investigation of American Ethnology" to the first meeting of the Board of Regents of the Smithsonian Institution just organized at Washington. In it he sketched the field of the new science of ethnology, as cultural anthropology is sometimes called. It was to include evidence from archeology as well as field studies and to use the methods of the exact sciences. The divisions of the proposed study covered all of the arts, crafts, customs, ideas and institutions which are a part of culture. In this small pamphlet he can truly be said to have laid down the fundamentals of the new science as it has been carried on since his day.

Schoolcraft's second wife worked faithfully as his literary helper, copying and filing his papers. She managed to make friends with Janee, but John always resented her. Schoolcraft put out a popular book, *Notes on the Iroquois*, and, in 1847, was appointed special agent in the Office of Indian Affairs, at a salary of $1,600 a year. His financial difficulties were now relieved and he was free to begin an extended work for which he moved to Washington in order to have access to the files of the Indian Office. Janee went along but John remained in New York where he was employed by a shipping company.

From now on Schoolcraft worked steadily on a many-volumed book which was to include everything he could bring together concerning North American Indians. His old mentor, Cass, had many years before sent out a questionnaire to missionaries and traders. It had brought in some useful material. Schoolcraft now repeated this method of gathering data. He, himself, had an immense amount of material. In fact, the shelves full of documents in the collection of the Library of Congress today are an indication of the careful way in which he preserved his papers. The existing mass of letters, papers, and notes is so extensive that one wonders if he ever threw away a piece of paper with anything written on it. An artist, Lieutenant Eastman, was engaged to make lithographs to illustrate the work, in some cases from the author's own sketches.

While working on this project, he also found time to write a campaign biography for Cass, who was now a middle-of-the-road politician on the issue of slavery. Cass believed that the federal government had no jurisdiction over the spread of slavery and that the new territories should decide for themselves. Martin Van Buren left the Democratic Party and ran on a free-soil platform supported by abolitionists and some radical Democrats. The conservative Democrats of the South, voting for the Whig candidate, the insignificant and half-educated General Taylor, helped elect him. Since Cass pleased neither group of extremists, Schoolcraft had the disappointment of seeing his old friend defeated.

In 1849, two family crises occurred. Janee was engaged to a young poet, Charles Fenno Hoffman. This young man had worked with her father in The New York Historical Society and shared his interest in Indians. A week before the wedding, the young man went insane and had to be put in an institution. Janee, who suffered from shock, was sent to Mary's relatives in South Carolina for a change of scene. Eventually she recovered and married.

The news from John in New York grew steadily worse. He borrowed large sums from friends of the family to spend on gambling and liquor. He was summoned to Washington where stormy scenes took place. Mary shut herself up in her room for three days and nights. Schoolcraft suffered from his disappointment as a father and from the emotional conflict. The tensions brought on a stroke which ended in an attack of paralysis, rendering his hands useless. He recovered to some extent, but it was the beginning of a lingering illness. After this date, his handwriting, which had always been neat and legible, became angular and scratchy, with many small blots as the pen caught in the paper.

In 1851, Schoolcraft published his *Memoirs of Thirty Years Residence with the Indian Tribes*, his liveliest and most colorful book. The first of six volumes of his government-commissioned project, *Historical and Statistical Information Concerning the Indians*, appeared the same year.

By now he was old and ill but, with Mary's help, he worked doggedly on his long book. Reduced to crutches and a wheelchair, he seldom got to the Indian Office or the War Office but did his writing at home. In spite of his infirmities, he managed to make one more trip to Detroit in 1858 to act as interpreter. It was a last meeting with the Indians and a sad one for the Indian Territory was fast vanishing, as the frontier moved west of the Mississippi. He was able to make the trip by means of the comparative luxury of the railroad. He wrote in his journal, "Where once they boiled their kettles of corn or thumped their magic drums they shall be seen no more. God help them in their wild wanderings!"

As far as his own work went, he was heartened by letters from Lewis Morgan who was now embarked on an ambitious work analyzing the social structure of the American Indian tribes. Another young man, Daniel C. Brinton, just graduated from Yale, wrote Schoolcraft in 1855, praising his many-volumed survey of the Indians. Brinton was to carry on the study of comparative mythology in America.

On the national scene, however, tragedy threatened. Cass, now secertary of state under Buchanan, wanted to strengthen the forts in Charleston harbor, since he thought war was inevitable. The secretaries of war, the treasury and the interior were southern sympathizers and fought against him. When Buchanan refused to act, Cass resigned his post on December 15, 1860. Five days later, South Carolina seceded. The history of the United States entered a new and violent phase. Janee's husband, who had been employed in Washington, left for Richmond and the Confederacy, taking her with him. Schoolcraft's wife, Mary, had just published a novel *The Black Gauntlet*, in which she violently defended the southern cause. John was now fighting with the Union forces.

Schoolcraft lay dying with tragedy and conflict all about him. He must have thought longingly of the old days at Sault, of the forest and his Indian friends of whom he wrote:

> *Oh how long shall I think of those bright silver lakes,*
> *And the scenes they exposed to thy view;*
> *My friends—and the wishes I formed for their sakes,*
> *And my bright yellow birchen canoe.*

He died on December 10, 1864, at seventy-two, having completed the notes for two more volumes he was unable to finish.

When we try to form a picture of Schoolcraft as a person, a man of great integrity emerges. Honest, conscientious, incredibly persevering and industrious, he left a large body of writing full of valuable anthropological data. His weakness as a scientist was lack of organization. His six-volume book, which he hoped would be his masterpiece, was filled with history, notes on customs, place names, artifacts, language, songs, legends, and biographies of famous chiefs. Unfortunately, there was no underlying plan, one thing follows another in no particular order. He had toyed with the idea that the American Indians were descendants of the legendary lost tribes of Israel, an idea current in his time. Although the efforts he made to compare Hebrew and Indian institutions were made on the basis of this farfetched theory, they nevertheless drew attention to the fact that there might be some similarity between ancient and preliterate forms of society. A most important activity, and one which anthropology did not undertake officially for centuries, was the task of mediating between preliterate and the modern industrial culture which we call civilization. The clash of these two kinds of cultures generally results in the destruction of the older one. Schoolcraft, by trying to help the American natives materially, and also by avoiding ignorant and destructive mistakes, was acting as the world's first applied anthropologist.

We think of the frontier hero as a tireless hunter, explorer, challenger of the hardships of the wilderness; he has come to assume a romantic character in American literature. While Schoolcraft did all these things, he seems curiously unheroic, conventionally pious, a little prim (when all around him were hard drinkers, he took only lemonade), self-consciously the literary man, who never rid himself of the sentimental and pedantic language of the second-rate New York poets of the period, a little pompous with certainly a touch of the schoolmaster. His letters to Mary Howard show, even in terms of the quaint conventions of the period, that he was romantic about women and idealized them profoundly. There is no doubt about his courage. He went among the Indians unafraid, secure in the knowledge that their word, once given, could be trusted. In all of his writing, he is modest and retiring, telling us little about his own feelings but now and then setting down colorful vignettes which show he was a good observer of other people.

One quotation from his memoirs will sum up the considered opinion concerning the Indians of this first American anthropologist, this Daniel Boone in spectacles. " 'What of the Indian character?,' a friend asked. 'I see them acting as other men would act, if placed exactly in their condition, prepared with the education the forest has given them and surrounded with the same wants, temptations, and dangers,' " was Schoolcraft's reply.

# ADOLF BASTIAN

The man who, with some justice, has been called the father of German anthropology, was born in 1825 and died in 1905; his name was Adolf Bastian. Contemporary with him were Gustav Klemm and Theodor Waitz. The first wrote a history of culture which appeared in ten volumes between 1843 and 1852, the second wrote a book on the anthropology of pre-literates, but both relied on material gathered from books by travellers, hunters, explorers and voyagers. They were what we might call "armchair anthropologists." Bastian, however, like Schoolcraft, did his travelling first hand and familiarized himself with peoples all over the world. Few men have been so tireless in roaming the earth. In the jungles of Africa, in the Buddhist kingdoms of Burma and Siam, in the coral islands of the Pacific, in the desert wastes of the east coast of South America, in China, Japan, the Celebes, Java, and Sumatra, Bastian appeared, notebook in hand, jotting down entries on customs, beliefs, legends.

We can perhaps find in his youth reasons for an international orientation. He was born in Bremen, the son of a well-known merchant. Bremen was an important harbor. From it, steamers set out with German manufactured goods to trade with other nations and to bring back raw materials from the colonial areas. The Bastian family had contacts in various parts of the world. Adolf's brother was already working in the house of Busing Schroeder & Co. in Singapore in 1865. No doubt, many foreigners visited the family and the boy must have often watched ships leaving the harbor and felt the urge to learn about the lands which appeared as different spots of color in the geography book. We know he was well grounded in languages for he handled English, French, Spanish and Portuguese with ease. The later part of his education was varied. He studied law at the University of Heidelberg and Berlin, biology at Jena and Würzburg, and took a degree in medicine in the University of Prague. In 1851, as soon as he graduated from Prague, he obtained a position as a ship's doctor on a schooner bound for Sydney, Australia. Thus he was launched on his career at the age of twenty-five. Like Schoolcraft, he was brilliant but, unlike the American, he had the luck to be born into a wealthy family, so that there was no problem about a college education and no lack of useful contacts to help him along in life.

Four years later, Bastian sailed from Capetown on the frigate of the admiral of the British fleet. Twenty-one guns greeted the ship as they put into the port of Luanda in what is now Angola. From here the twenty-nine-year-old scholar intended to visit the interior of the Congo. The local form of transportation was a hammock slung on a pole carried by two bearers. Reclining in this, Bastian traveled up the coast to Quinsembo, surrounded by noisy, naked black children begging for money.

The king of Quinsembo lived some distance from the coast and never came near the sea because it was believed that if he looked upon it, he would die and his kingdom would be destroyed. This was a tabu or magical rule established by the king's fetish. Bastian used the Portuguese term *fetiche*, from which we get "fetish," for what we would now call cult worship. A fetish was a holy object, an idol, or perhaps a pot with magical ingredients in it which contained a spirit whose wishes were interpreted by the priests of the cult. When Bastian was carried up in his hammock to visit the king, he found himself in a small plaza surrounded by mud huts, one of which was the king's palace. The whitewashed walls were decorated with figures of warriors and canoes, illustrating scenes from legends. A large tamarind tree stood in the center of the plaza and a wooden statue leaned against it. With great difficulty the king's armchair was brought out of the palace which was nearly knocked down in the process. The ruler wore a red uniform and tight uncomfortable white trousers which he seemed unused to. When he was seated, a feathered three-cornered hat was ceremoniously placed on his head.

As soon as he was enthroned, all the assembled subjects clapped. Bastian spoke to him in pidgin English which was used by traders along the coast. He announced that he had come "to look at the king's face and hoped his belly was well." Presents of rum and calico were given while the subjects clapped loudly at the beginning and end of every sentence. When the audience was over, Bastian was carried off by his bearers at a dead run in his wildly swinging hammock.

For his trip into the Congo Bastian needed eight bearers to take turns carrying the hammock, twelve for his baggage and a headman to interpret and take charge of the expedition. For this post he engaged a former factory worker who had been dismissed for stealing. The Europeans said Bastian was insane to choose a desperate character who would surely cut his throat. The anthropologist's formula for dealing with the ex-criminal was to trust him completely, now and then remind

him of white "superiority," while respecting the African's beliefs and prejudices. In the end, the trip cost half what he had
expected. His method of treating the Africans worked everywhere. Bastian found his headman intelligent and he stuck to
the motto that he would rather employ a clever rascal than an
honorable idiot.

Since the rainy season was about to begin, it was not the
best time for travelling. After passing the village of Impambu,
where he was greeted by red and yellow painted fetish wor-
shippers with tigerskins about their middles, he made some
progress up the river and at night hung his hammock between
two trees. In the morning, a thin rain awoke him. Presently
a whirlwind struck, blowing hammock, bearers and baggage
into a heap. Then a tropical downpour soaked everyone to the
skin. Some bearers became discouraged and deserted but
Bastian was able to replace them with boys from Impambu.

When they reached a fetish hut, the bearers refused to go
near it. Bastian got out of his hammock and, over their pro-
tests that he was going to his death, insisted on entering. The
temple had three wood-framed doors and was covered with
straw matting, the doorposts being painted with green and
yellow figures. Inside he found nothing but a heap of earth
with three red and white striped wooden forks stuck into it.
In this area, the cult of the god Dambu was dominant.

At the next village, Bastian fainted and realized that he had
come down with malaria. His bearers triumphantly pointed out
that he had touched the fetish temple and was therefore
doomed. They expected to bury him by nightfall. Bastian,
however, had no intention of allowing himself to be buried,
and in three days was over his attack of fever. He then had
an audience with the local king who sang a song in his honor
accompanied by a chorus of courtiers. In this area, there had
originally been a clan system (extended family groups headed

by more or less elected chiefs), which had given way to local kings with the power of life and death over their subjects, any of whom they had the right to enslave. This situation was generally true of West Africa and the habit of enslaving prisoners of war made it easy for the Portuguese to obtain human goods for the American market.

In June 1857, Bastian was in Capetown, South Africa, and from there undertook a trip to the East coast of the continent, which is described in his first book, *Ein Besuch nach San Salvador* (A Visit to San Salvador) which was published two years later, the same date as Darwin's *Origin of Species*. In the preface he explained that he was interested in comparing customs and ideas. The subtitle, *A Contribution to Mythology and Psychology* shows that he had already begun the study that was to be the primary interest of his career. Since anthropology was not yet a recognized science, he, too, had to create it as he went along. His books (and in spite of his activity as a traveller he managed to turn out more than ten thousand printed pages) lack organization. Sections of travel description are often lively and full of shrewd insights. Volumes which deal with comparative customs and mythology ramble on and on. Long theoretical prefaces set forth his ideas about anthropology and, in some cases, when he grows philosophical, he is fairly obscure.

The San Salvador book, however, has much to tell us about conditions in west and central Africa in the middle of the nineteenth century. Portugal was the first European country, under its famous ruler Henry the Navigator, to undertake extensive exploration in little-known parts of the world. Both Africa and South America were areas of Portuguese colonization. When Portuguese Diego Ciao discovered the mouth of the Congo River in 1483, four Portuguese ambassadors were sent to Uzimgo, the head chief of Manicongo, which was in

the interior of Africa. When they were detained by the African
chief, Ciao seized four Africans and took them home to Portugal as hostages. The prisoners were made to feel the wealth
and importance of Portugal and thus turned out to be inter-
mediaries in the relationships between the Europeans and the
Africans. On his return trip, three or four years later, Diego
brought presents to Uzimgo and succeeded in converting him
to Christianity. He agreed to send some of his people to Portugal to be trained in European ways. In return the Portuguese
monarch sent three ships carrying priests, skilled workers and
tools. The aims of the Portuguese at this point were to form
an alliance and to convert the natives. The Portuguese, who
viewed everything through imperial spectacles, saw the Manicongo chief as an African emperor. Actually, although he
headed a loose confederation of tribes, his authority could not
be compared to that of a European emperor and the Congo
peoples were not sufficiently developed beyond the stage of
hunting and village agriculture for there to be any unifying
administration. At any rate, the first intentions of the Europeans were reasonably constructive. They hoped to create an
alliance with Nzinga, the son of Uzimgo, and to turn his
imaginary empire into a Christian country which would be
of value to Portugal.

Unfortunately, during the reign of Nzinga's son, Alfonso
I, the slave trade had already begun. The Europeans
needed workers for the Portuguese plantations in what is now
Brazil, and the Africans were accustomed to enslaving prisoners of war. Alfonso, officially a Christian, was well educated
in the Portuguese language and traditions, while the rest of
the country was pagan. In addition, his underchiefs, particularly those of the island of São Tomé, went into the slave
trade. Missionaries sent to the Congo also turned into slave
traders and Alfonso's pathetic requests that the Portuguese

king replace these corrupt subjects were unheeded. A shadowy court tried to imitate the protocol and behavior of the Europeans. Meanwhile São Tomé became the most important slave port on the African coast and the Portuguese bishop, who made it his seat, encouraged the traffic in human beings.

Probably there were no more than two hundred Europeans in Africa in the sixteenth century. Some married Negro wives; in this respect they did not practice racial discrimination, and their children became corrupt priests and slave traders until the white strain was gradually bred out. The Portuguese colony also suffered from the invasion of a cannibalistic tribe, the Jagas. Catholic missions came and went, leaving few traces behind them. Capuchins came from Rome and performed baptisms and marriages wholesale, 340,000 of the first, 50,000 of the second. But, by 1700, the twelve churches of San Salvador were in ruins. The Congo was no more than a hunting ground for slaves, and this detestable commerce had destroyed whatever good intentions had first motivated the European explorers. Today, the disturbed state of the Congo and the seething discontent of Angola are the heritage of Europe's first great colonial adventure. Bastian knew his history and, with his interest in preliterate people, was anxious to see for himself what results almost four hundred years of contact between the Portuguese and Africans had produced. It was for this reason that he was willing to endure the difficult life of the interior.

On and on, swaying in his hammock, Bastian travelled through the tropical rain. After traversing many hills and valleys, his bearers climbed to the isolated plateau which held the so-called capital of the Portuguese colony. São Salvador, as it is called in proper Portuguese, consisted of a group of huts, built on a plain that was covered with grass as tall as a man, and ringed by mountains fluted with ravines. On the

whitewashed walls of the mud huts were colored murals of
soldiers and, appropriately, rows of slaves. The grass was so
high that it hid the huts and the pattern of streets was lost
among tall palm trees that spread over the courtyards. Now
and then the green was broken by gaily colored flowerbeds.
Around the city were fields of corn and wheat. (One of the
positive Portuguese achievements was the introduction of
maize, manioc, citrus fruits and potatoes from their colonies
in Brazil.) Among the palm trees the broken arches of ruined
chapels and of several churches rose from the grass, the only
visible remains of the unfulfilled imperial dreams of the
Portuguese.

Bastian was given several huts for his party and was immediately visited by Dom Antonio and Dom Domingo, sons
of the king who had just died. The farce of Portuguese
royalty was still kept up, all of the reigning family had
high-sounding names in addition to their African ones. In the
fifteenth century, when the colonizers were creating black
counts and marquises, the royal patent was indicated by
branding the arms of Portugal on their shoulders with a red-
hot iron. Apparently no one saw the irony of the parallel with
the branding of slaves.

The two princes informed Bastian that they were scholars
and could read. One of them drew from a leather portfolio
the tattered remnants of a book, which turned out to be some
loose leaves from a Latin prayerbook plus a few holy pictures.
Adjusting his spectacles, which had lost their lenses and kept
slipping off his nose, Dom Domingo failed to read any of the
Latin, but, when Bastian gave him a Portuguese book, he
made out a couple of isolated words. In all the Portuguese
colony this was the extent of the educational system set up by
European rule. (There has been shockingly little progress
since.)

Bastian was visited by the regent's son; the regent was an older relative who ruled because the heir was not of age. Bastian got drunk with him and later had an audience with the crown prince who wore a blue uniform with white trousers and sat under a red, yellow, and blue umbrella. On this occasion, Bastian gave his royal friends a short talk on world trade, urging them to deal with the British and also not to forget the Germans.

On the way back to the coast, the indomitable ethnologist had another attack of fever. While he was trying to recover from it in a native village, the wails of a newborn baby prompted some reflections upon the custom which was to be called *couvade*. Strangely enough, this was a rite in which, when the mother was about to give birth, the father went to bed and pretended to be indisposed. Since childbirth was a time of danger during which infections often destroyed the mother or the child at birth, Bastian wondered if the father were not trying to ward off the evil spirits of disease by attracting them to himself.

The motion of the hammock made him feel worse when he resumed his journey and he could not endure rubber waterproof clothing on account of the heat. He envied his naked bearers to whom the rain was nothing but he was part of the Victorian era and the idea of adopting the native lack of clothing was foreign to him. He suffered in respectability.

At the mines of Pembe, he decided to travel with an armed caravan which was transporting copper to the coast. He set off with eighty soldiers and three hundred and fifty bearers, carrying loads of copper ore on their heads in baskets. Each basket had a pole projecting in front so that, when the bearer wanted to unload, he could incline his head and rest the pole on the ground.

Unfortunately, the caravan was attacked by hostile natives.

All was in confusion, poor Bastian had to leap from his hammock and run for his life. The caravan broke through the ambush, however, and pushed on. Back at Impambu, where the party was so ferociously tortured by mosquitos that neither he nor his bearers could sleep, the Negroes decided to pass the night dancing. To the accompaniment of a marimba, maracas and beaten pots, a solo dancer performed a kind of pantomime while a chorus sat in a circle, shouting and clapping. Each dance ended with cries of "Zimba, Zimba!" Later the performance turned into "an obscene cancan" which, he had to admit, except for the lack of costume "was not much worse than the scenes which formerly could be seen in certain public halls in Berlin."

Bastian's connection with the arts was, however, remote. Toward the end of his life, a friend asked him when he had last been to a play. He said "in 1859." When then had he been to an art exhibition? "Never," he replied. The British and French had agreed to suppress the slave trade but since this was before the Civil War, the American market still existed. The Portuguese consequently carried on the traffic in human beings. Americans, who had technically abandoned it, kept a Portuguese or Spanish flag aboard ship and gave their command over to one of these nationalities when they carried a cargo of slaves. The Negroes, Bastian concluded, were better off in their original condition, for Europe, self-appointed apostle of civilization to the world, had brought them only firearms, firewater and slavery.

Bastian finished his book with a long appendix on comparative mythology. The copious quotes from other travellers and scholars, which appear in all of his work, show that he did his homework carefully and familiarized himself with everything written about a country before he visited it.

In 1860, he published his three-volume *Der Mensch in der*

*Geschichte* (Man in History). In it he set forth his basic ideas. Unfortunately, when he became theoretical, his style became very long-winded and he often failed to state his position clearly and logically or fully define his main theme. Impatient with German philosophy, which he considered subjective, he felt that scholars would be better occupied in trying to understand the psychology of various types of social groups.

Religion was the key to man's psychology. The soul always sought for unity and expressed it in terms of its material environment. The preliterate, not distinguishing between the world outside and the world of fantasy within his mind, tried to connect his personal feeling with external events.

The notions of omens was basic. If a man fell into a river and was saved by catching hold of an overhanging twig, the episode would make a great impression on him. Ordinary cause and effect would not satisfy him as an explanation of such an important event. The man's feelings took on great significance; he projected them into the object that had saved him. The twig acquired power and importance and mystical qualities. This might even cause him to think there was something living, an unseen spirit within it. In a similar way, a boy clung to a lucky marble with which he had won many games. This, Bastian believed, was the psychology of fetishism. Upon it mythology could be developed, and gods in human form created. Religions which developed in this way could be changed by contacts between people. Reactions to a foreign culture were determined by the stage of development a people had reached before the contact. Very early in its history, a group could passively accept a more complicated or "higher" culture. A primitive group which was already worshipping a stone, for instance, and then was taught by another group to worship the stars, would for a long time connect its new worship with its old. Bastian's book piled up all the phenomena of preliterate religion, which he had himself gathered and which he had collected from books, on a comparative basis.

Behind all of Bastian's thinking is the idea of the basic unity of mankind, a similarity of custom and belief. In this he was not alone. Darwin's hypothesis of evolution was not an isolated idea. The most inquiring minds of the period were all trying to organize the new facts of science into a unified view of the world. In the past, the master system had been an organized religion. Bastian (and many other scientists) could no longer accept any single religious system. The following quote indicates the direction of his thinking: "We no longer endure the tyrannical whims of a jealous god. We are no longer afraid that a mighty enemy will fling our protector out of the heavens. We humble ourselves no more before the fearful drama in which the almighty creator must sacrifice himself in order to avert disaster from the world." In other words, western man could not accept Greek or Christian myths literally. He went on: "We depend upon no alien help, for all such help is deceitful, we lean on no staff for every staff can rot and splinter."

Thus far in rejecting supernatural ideas, Bastian is outlining a position not far from what is now called existentialism. "The yoke is broken and we are free. Free as the bird in the air or the fish in the water, free as the tree in the open meadow . . . and what does the heart of man seek? To know the whole of which he is an integral part." The answer to this wish seems to indicate that Bastian was somewhat influenced by Buddhism, of which he made a serious study. "Can he hope to understand it in any other way than through the medium of his participation in the general wholeness? Can he hope for a more certain or more lofty consolation than to know himself an atom in timelessness and eternity? The scientific horizon of legend and myth is torn asunder by natural science. Do our eyes lie when they stare into eternity? Seek to become timeless yourself. If you are surrounded by eternity, soon thoughts, ideas will well up in the eternity of the All. You will feel yourself putting down roots into the laws of the cosmic harmony. With it you will grow ceaselessly and endlessly, as it grows, and you will fulfill yourself in conscious harmony."

What Bastian is saying, in his rather romantic style, is that for him the sense of scientific laws, permeating the world and enduring without end, gives him a mystical feeling of unity and satisfies his wish for an organized view of life. It was this search for unity which sent him tirelessly scouring the earth for more and more ethnic facts, insatiably examining culture after culture for the fundamental psychological ideas which he felt were the key to the behavior of human beings.

In 1861, he set off for eastern Asia, a journey that was to last four years and result in a six-volume account, which included both his travel experiences and his study of the Buddhist religion. His adventure with the king of Burma is perhaps the most colorful episode in his life.

England, the major colonial power in the nineteenth century, always pushing into the Orient in order to achieve various types of domination and protective control, had annexed Burma's coastal provinces and, although hostilities between the two countries had ceased, the peace treaty had not yet been signed. Burma was an absolute monarchy, a true Oriental despotism where the Buddhist religion was supreme and Europeans were not particularly welcome.

On a beautiful afternoon in October, Bastian's ship sailed into the Irrawaddy River, entering a busy harbor full of Burmese in tall, pointed straw hats sailing small fishing boats or poled bamboo rafts. The ship proceeded upstream between carefully tilled fields, passed the silver tip of a pagoda that shimmered in the sun above a wood of dark-leaved trees, and after another turn in the river, came upon the colossal magnificence of the pagoda of Rangoon which rose high above the rows of mud huts which made up the city. As the river was the high road to Mandalay, Bastian got himself a Burmese houseboat, equipped with four oarsmen and a pilot. The boat had a mast with a matting sail; in front of it was his dining room, enclosed by matting, and behind it his bedroom. He engaged a cook who tutored him in the language and literature of the country.

Bastian described the Burmese as slender, tawny, attractive people who tattooed their skins. Burmese women, when they bathed, stepped out of their loincloths, and Bastian remarked that the true tint of the skin could be seen on the hips and loins which were as light as those of Europeans.

The Burmese, as good Buddhists, would not shed blood. Fishermen faced with this dilemma of respecting life, left their newly caught fish to gasp and die in the sun. If they could not breathe air, it was not the fault of the fishermen.

When Bastian reached Mandalay and was preparing to continue on north, he was suddenly visited by officials of the king who told him his passport was no longer valid and that he must leave his houseboat and take up residence on the shore. This was a sad blow. He wrote a letter to the king, saying he had many valuables on his boat and could not leave it. The officials wanted to take him with them, not his letter, but he put them off the boat by force. They returned shortly, summoning him to an audience with the king.

On reaching the palace, he had to leave his shoes outside. He was conducted into a small audience hall with pillars decorated in red and gold. Stairs mounted to a balustrade at one end. The courtiers sat on the floor looking toward the stairs.

The king came through a door opening on the balcony and sat down on a divan placed on the top step of the stairs. The courtiers put their hands together and threw themselves face down on the floor where they remained on elbows and knees.

Bastian contented himself with nodding. Feet were supposed to be hidden from the king, on esthetic grounds; Bastian, squatting, made efforts to fulfill the demands of etiquette. The king, in rich silks encrusted with gold ornaments, surrounded by his young children, stared at Bastian for a time and finally asked the purpose of his trip. There was a distinct atmosphere of intrigue and menace which made Bastian feel he had to be careful. He replied that, as a European, he wished to know foreign countries and to study their religions. Burma was ideal for the study of Buddhism at its purest.

This pleased the king who asked him how long he intended to stay. Bastian made the mistake of saying that he wanted to travel in the north and visit ancient shrines. The king told him tartly that it was impossible to travel and study at the same time and that he did not think Bastian was telling the truth. Because of his recent troubles with the English, the king may well have suspected the German of being a spy. With all the European countries pushing into the less developed areas of the world and annexing large territories, he could scarcely be blamed for his suspicions.

For a time they both sat silent and looked at each other. Finally, the king said, "There is no better place than Burma for the study of Buddhism, in Burma no better place than Mandalay, and in Mandalay no better place than my palace. There is plenty of room for you in the palace. I shall send for books and a teacher. Is your answer yes or no?"

Bastian knew very well that any utterance of the king's was a royal command to be obeyed without question. The answer had to be yes. His friends among the merchants in Mandalay watched him pack and disappear into the palace, sadly assuring him he would never come out again. The record of poisonings and mysterious disappearances connected with life among the king's entourage was not such as to be very encouraging. When Bastian was installed in his quarters, a learned scholar came to teach him Buddhism. The king commanded that he first study Burmese thoroughly, then the ancient Pali (the old Indian language of the Buddhist scripts), finally the holy books. Bastian insisted on reversing the process. The poor professor was in a constant state of terror for fear the king would find out that his orders had not been obeyed.

The ethnologist was again received by the king, this time in the great audience hall. Luckily there were some gifts heaped in front of Bastian so that he was able to hide his feet politely. The king preached a while on the importance of a Buddhist's refusal to destroy life. Bastian asked if it was permitted to defend one's own life. The king said no, such a crude idea would lead to the killing of insects (fleas existed in the palace of The Golden-Footed One). After the king unsuccessfully tried to make Bastian reject the heresy of self-defense, he ordered some parrots brought in, in a golden cage. As an example to the flea-killing heathen, he ceremoniously freed them to show his respect for life. Bastian privately reflected that they could quite easily be caught in the next room and used for another parable.

Bastian was again dismissed and a few weeks later, as he industriously studied Buddhism, the reason for his polite imprisonment became clear. While in Mandalay, he had taken some wax from a child's ear and improved the child's hearing. The mother had visited a friend in the king's harem. Rumors concerning Bastian had raced through the harem and finally through the court until they reached the king. Now several courtiers came to him with ear ailments. All he did was syringe their ears with water but they insisted they had benefited tremendously. Bastian finally got tired of a stream of patients and prescribed mustard plasters. It had gradually dawned on him that the king, hearing he was a foreign doctor, and hearing good things of European medicine, had decided that a doctor was what he needed in his court. Since Burmese medicine was in the stage of witch doctors and magic, the king was actually motivated by rather progressive ideas. Bastian, however, did not plan to spend the rest of his life as physician in residence at the court of Burma.

Now an indirect struggle began between the stubborn German scientist and the Oriental potentate who had never before in his life been opposed. Bastian felt he must somehow put a halt to his medical practice. Conveniently he had lost his medicine chest. The king summoned him to an audience and asked him to give the harem beauties medicine. Bastian insisted that he had none.

He was told that, "medicine or no medicine, the king commands."

Bastian refused.

Such a thing had never been heard of. The king's son stamped his foot, rustling his silks under his gold umbrella. He had become rather friendly with Bastian, but this ended their relationship. An icy chill invaded the atmosphere of the court. This lasted for eight days. It was generally expected that the German would mysteriously disappear. "Fear" wrote Bastian calmly, "is useless and in this case it would have been dangerous." His teacher came to him trembling and pathetically asked him if he perhaps knew how to make gold. This might distract and appease the king.

One evening a detachment of troops marched into his quarters. The officers looked at him sternly as if about to arrest him. Bastian blandly asked them to be seated and questioned them about Buddhism. They stared at him, astonished. Without a word, they marched out again.

The ladies of the harem, whom Bastian had treated, begged for' more medicine. Bastian made this an excuse to go into the city. He was stopped at the gate by a sentry. He made a disturbance, insisted on seeing the king's son, who had been avoiding him, and shouted that he was a guest, not a prisoner. The prince made excuses, but Bastian was still not allowed to leave the palace. He realized that there was no European he could appeal to, not even a consul. His house arrest cut him off completely from the outside world. The scientist courageously sat it out and suddenly the king's mood changed; the courtiers smiled on the ethnologist. Once more, they came to sing, dance, drink his tea and smoke his cigarettes.

He struck while the iron was hot and demanded permission to leave. He got it, a passport written on a long palm leaf that could be conveniently rolled up. It was sealed with the king's seal. The traveller drew a long breath and continued on his way.

He next penetrated the jungles of Siam (present-day Thailand) seated on the back of an elephant. He hired four of these forest giants with wild tribesmen, called Karens, as guides. By day they travelled through teak forests; each night his forest people built him a little house of bamboo, in which his sleep was disturbed by the yells of monkeys.

At Bangkok, he saw the installation as a cultural symbol of the sacred white elephant, emblem of the country, to be seen on the flag and, at one time, on Siamese stamps. Although the scientist was invited by the king of Siam to witness an elephant fight (elephants maddened by picador-like lance thrusts were made to tear down barricades) he had no difficulties with him such as he had had with the Burmese sovereign.

At the end of this trip he had visited not only Burma and Siam but also Cambodian temples. He then took a Dutch warship which carried him to Yokohama, Shanghai, Tientsin, Peking, parts of Mongolia and Siberia. He returned to Bremen in 1866 to write his book, entitled *The Peoples of East Asia*. Previously, he had been made assistant director of the imperial ethnological museum of Berlin for, by then, he had made his mark as a pioneer of the new science.

Germany, which had come late into the race for colonies, went in for societies for the study of geography. Out of these came the Society for the Exploration of Equatorial Africa, which was, of course, a high-sounding name for an organization which would be used to investigate potential colonies. Bastian's next trip, which took place in 1873, was financed by this society. The purpose of the expedition, on which he was to be joined by two other scholars, was to explore the Luanda coast.

He took a Portuguese steamer from Lisbon which, after stopping at one or two islands, put ashore in the bay of Kabinda but unfortunately ran on a rock. The machinist who might have repaired the leak was down with fever. The sailors pumped desperately and when the vessel was in danger of sinking, finally ran it on a sand bar. The trading post on the shore was run by the Dutch and called Banano. It manufactured palm oil which was shipped to Europe. The method of obtaining workers was typical of European-African relations. The Dutch paid taxes to local chiefs who, in turn, forced their people to work for the foreigners without pay.

While he waited for the other members of the expedition to arrive, Bastian took trips along the coast, visiting Portuguese and Dutch trading posts in his perambulating hammock. There was a multitude of small states, some of which were Portuguese protectorates, ruled over by petty but absolute chiefs. The terrain consisted sometimes of sand but sometimes the bearers were forced inland by broken rocky capes. At times rivers had to be crossed in which the bearers waded breast deep, resting the poles of the hammock on their heads.

When he travelled northward through the tall grass, he often saw fires lit in the underbrush. This was a method of hunting used by the natives by which they drove the game into nets.

Along the route he encountered an *ilongo,* or shrine, which he wanted to visit, as usual against the advice of his men. It contained animal skulls sacred to an earth spirit which regulated the growth of plants. At first, the natives insisted the sight of it would strike him dead. Then they objected that the spirit would be angered by the presence of the white man and spoil the harvest. Since these tabus were strongly felt, he gave in and allowed them to lead him to the Makisso Umpindi as a substitute. This was a dried-up tree trunk with a thatch of straw over it where, on certain special times, spirits were raised. Even here, to offset the visit of the European, a dance was performed and the village elder called upon those women and girls who were particularly in touch with sexual fertility and the vegetation spirit to take part. The head musician took his place at a long drum beaten with the hand. At this a *ganga,* or priest, began to sing, the women sprang and danced about the tree trunk, always presenting their buttocks to it and these portions of their anatomy were loudly smacked by the priest to indicate the end of the ceremony. In front of a house full of magical objects, Bastian saw a pot under a straw thatch with a bundle of leaves in front of it. This stood for the fetish, Bumba. An object such as this was often invoked to bring rain. Another type of fetish was a pot adorned with horns; in front of it a wooden idol, with a mirror on its breast, was stuck in the ground.

In another village a procession carried the images of two gods. One, made of wood, had a mirror and a sword hung upon it. Its name was Umkwanje. Simbuka, the other idol, had nails driven into it for magical purposes. Its face was made of clay with eyes and ears painted upon it. Both images were carried by tattooed slaves.

In a house in one of the villages, Bastian saw a coffin with a drum beside it. The widower, smeared with ashes, sat near. When his period of mourning was over, he was forbidden to put on new clothes until he had bathed in the sea.

A girl, about to be married, was made to sit in a special hut, her skin painted red. For days she was visited by an old woman who instructed her in the duties of a wife. Bastian also discovered that a wife, whose husband had fallen ill, had been forced to drink poison because she had been accused of bewitching him. The fact that she survived proved her innocence. This observation has been fully corroborated and elaborated by later ethnologists. The idea that illness is due to hostile magic is widespread and causes, in some tribes, an actual paranoia. Witch doctors specialize in identifying the criminals. The same basic belief, of course, motivated the witch trials in Massachusetts. The ordeal by poison mentioned by Bastian is arranged by selecting a poison that is not quite strong enough to kill a rather healthy person. Thus the accused has a fifty-fifty chance of surviving and, of course, if he or she is innocent, the spirits will throw their weight into the balance. Further on, in still another village, Bastian discovered the body of a chief, surrounded by the dead man's worldly goods, as it was being cremated on a sort of gridiron. Ceremonial talks between a trader and a nearby ruler were taking place. The prince, whose name was Massanje, was followed by a group of nobles, sword bearers who painted their eyes yellow and a black line across their foreheads. As in other such cases of public interchange, at the end of each speech by the prince, they repeated his last word in chorus. When an important point was made, one of them stuck his sword in the ground. Once the talk was over, there was a distribution of rum, festal fires were lit and the night was given over to dancing.

The banks of Chiloango River were thick with tropic vegetation surmounted by tall palms. Monkeys played in the tree-tops; it was a country of chimpanzees and gorillas. On the exposed clay shores, gigantic crocodiles sunned themselves. At a town by the name of Chicambo, Bastion had the opportunity of watching a witch doctor treating a sick man. The patient's face had been painted, the nose red, the forehead yellow, cheeks black. Into a fire, burning in front of the hut, magic bundles were thrown. At one side, a row of idols was set up. A chorus of women sang monotonously whereupon the witch doctor began to whirl, faster and faster, until he was stamping madly. He grew wilder and wilder, leaping over the fire, the fetish pots and even the spectators, ending by rushing out blindly into the darkness. Later, he returned and circled the hut, waving a flaming torch. His assistant, who had been sitting on a stool, first went into convulsions and then froze into immobility while the singing went on and on. Presently the assistant began to question the spirit who was supposed to have entered the hut. The chorus answered. When the details of the cause of the disease were known, the doctor and his assistant danced again, to be joined by a third magician who leaped wildly with a burning torch.

The morning after this exhausting treatment, the patient got up and went to work. The cause of his illness was diagnosed satisfactorily as his having eaten a totemically forbidden food. This meant that the animal connected with his tribal group, either as a protector or an ancestor, was tabu, but the unfortunate patient had broken the tabu by eating it. The

treatment was not yet at an end, however, because the following day, the physicians consulted and changed the diag-
nosis. They decided that the suffering man's soul had been
detached from his body by a recently deceased neighbor. (All
over Africa and in many other parts of the world it is still
believed that the dead can cause illness.) This meant that the
treatment would have to go on for days. Bastian wrote ironi-
cally that it would also extract from the patient his last cent.
In this area a trader told Bastian that people had been burnt
as witches for causing sickness.

Near Luanda, Bastian was shocked to see a Negro hanging
head down from a tree while all the worthies of the village
stood around him shouting. There was a great crowd and a
great deal of noise. The story illustrated still another African
belief. A leopard had killed a woman of the village. When the
most important landowner set out to hunt the animal down,
unfortunately, he himself was killed. The ganga decreed that
it was no ordinary leopard but a were-leopard, a man able
to turn himself into a leopard, a particularly dangerous type
of witch. The man hanging in the tree had been identified by
the ganga as the criminal. He had been given the ordeal by
poison but the results had not been considered to be conclu-
sive. The torture went on to Bastian's dismay. He spoke to
a trader, but was told that nothing could be done. The belief
in the ability of certain persons to turn themselves into preda-
tory animals exists in many places, there were supposed to
be werewolves in Europe and were-tigers in Malaysia. Also,
in the late nineteenth century, there were a number of societies in Africa known as Leopard Men. Murders were committed by them under the pretense that their members were
were-leopards.

On Bastian's visit to Angoy, a town near Luanda, he was
having breakfast with one of the king's counsellors when he

again heard a disturbance in the center of the village. His men told him not to go out of the hut but he was bound to satisfy his curiosity. When he went outside, he saw what at first seemed a formless mass of palm leaves but he then made out the colossal inhuman mask above it. There were several of these figures dancing madly and lashing about them with whips. The spectators shrank away and gave them a wide berth. These figures, which sprang and stamped threateningly, were Sindunga, soldiers of the king. They belonged to a secret society, which was used by the ruler to carry out his commands, which sometimes even included murder. Such societies exist in Africa today, and their activities vary from carrying out religious rites to actual terrorism.

The various customs which Bastian recorded on this trip are testimony to the accuracy of his observation and his alertness as an investigator of anthropological data. His great contemporary, the English anthropologist Sir Edward Tyler, once stated admiringly that whenever he took trouble to verify Bastian's facts, they turned out to be correct.

Bastian's next journey, undertaken in 1875, is of particular interest because it included South and Central America, important areas for the study of American archeology. The trip was financed by the Berlin museum in order for Bastian to collect specimens from the ancient cultures. He sailed from Liverpool, and on May 23, he glimpsed a strip of sand with a grey overcast above it, which he was told was the coast of Brazil.

Quarantine regulations, which required a stay of some days before foreigners were allowed into the country, did not allow him to visit either the ports of Bahia or Buenos Aires. He commented, however, on the fact that Brazil was ridden with yellow fever, which he attributed to the damp climate and "miasma-filled air," while Buenos Aires (Good Airs) was well

named, since the atmosphere of the city, at the mouth of the
great Rio Plata, was clear and fresh. This was an illustration
of the medical beliefs of the period. Miasmas, which were
supposed to cause illness, were envisioned as harmful vapors
which arose from the damp areas. It took another quarter of
a century before the dampness was linked up with marshes in
which mosquitos, the carriers of yellow fever, bred.

The passage through the Straits of Magellan was something
of an adventure for a steamer, for sailing ships it had been
hazardous. Bastian stayed up all night to watch. The straits
were full of rocky islands and reefs; on both sides of the passage, in the gloomy night, black masses of rock loomed threateningly. The ship threaded its way through the openings
between them. There seemed to be no end to the stony senti-
nels and the intricacies of the channel. Now and then natives
in canoes were seen or cries were heard from the shore where
fires flickered. It was from such beacons that the large island
at the end of South America had received its name Tierra
del Fuego (Land of Fire). Some of the land masses rose up
into actual snow-covered peaks and in the folds of the mountains there were glaciers. Soundings had to be taken constantly
as the vessel worked its way to the Pacific, through the tor-
tuous channels. Many of these were so narrow that the big
English steamers could not get through. Knowing of the many
wrecks which still occurred, Bastian was glad to be travelling
on a narrow-beamed German ship.

When they anchored briefly, some French colonists who
had been living in the area, came aboard. Bastian immediately
questioned them about the customs of the natives. He was told
that they lived mostly on guanaco (a kind of wild llama) and
rats, which inhabited the underbrush. Fire was made by rubbing two sticks together. Meat was either eaten raw or cooked
over hot coals. These people, who did not possess even pot-

tery, hardened their wooden lancetips in the fire and topped their arrows with chipped flints. An interesting example of acculturation was taking place (one culture changing another). When they could get pieces of broken bottles, they applied the chipping technique, used on flints, to the new material, made glass arrowheads, and bound them to the haft with sinews and glue made of resin. These tribes did not even build houses. They hollowed out small holes under bushes and lay pressed close together against the cold. Fuegians wore no clothes whatsoever except guanaco skins as cloaks, or thrown around them as blankets, and sinews strung with mussel shells or stones around the neck, arms and legs. Bastian was told that the women, who shaved off their hair, offered their breasts to strangers to suck as a sign of hospitality.

The primitive simplicity of these unfortunate people was the cause of their extinction. Missionaries, who arrived at the end of the nineteenth century, were shocked by their lack of clothes. Since these natives also fished and were constantly in and out of cold water, the misguided efforts of the missionaries to dress them in European clothes proved fatal. Once dressed, the natives went about constantly soaked to the skin. In about twenty years, they succumbed to bronchial diseases and tuberculosis. Today, there are no Fuegians.

Concerning their religion, all Bastian learned was that stone images had been seen on a flat platform, images in the form of a cross, a sun, a half moon and a hand.

The straits safely passed, the steamer reached the coast of southern Chile. This area had been inhabited by the Araucanians, a hardy tribe which put up a valiant fight against the Spanish.

Bastian, concentrating on comparative mythology and basic concepts, cited a myth which described the Araucanian warriors who died in the fight against the Spaniards as having been carried off to a land beyond the sea by a great whale. In times of crisis, they would return through the milky way to help their brother warriors who were still resisting. This reminded Bastian of the Teutonic Valkyries who carried off the German fallen heroes. It seemed to him an example of what he termed "elementary ideas," that is, basic ideas which were bound to arise in certain states of culture in similar environments.

At Valparaiso, he left the ship and took the railway to Santiago, known as the Paris of America. He noted that the railroad was a remarkable feat of engineering. Its builder was an American, Henry Meiggs, who had perpetrated a great fraud in city finances in San Francisco. He then chartered a ship and left hurriedly with his ill-gotten gains, pursued ineffectually by the police. He arrived in Chile, where he could not be extradited to the United States, and proceeded to reveal himself as, if not an honest railroad builder (public finances were habitually conducted with fraud and embezzlement in South America), at least an extremely capable one. The Chilean line swooped through the mountains, over viaducts and through tunnels, to the admiration of the native Chileans whose efforts at railroad engineering had not gotten beyond the talking stage. Later, Meiggs was to build the Lima-Huancayo line, which was also a great achievement for it spirals up through the sierras to nearly fifteen hundred feet. These two lines are today still the only important railways on the west coast of South America, for that continent entered the age of the airplane without going through the railroad era.

In passing through the straits and up the coast of South America Bastian was retracing some of Darwin's voyage in the *Beagle*. He noted that, in 1832, when Darwin wanted to enter churches in Santiago, the bigoted clergy prevented him for they did not consider the Protestant Darwin a Christian.

The atmosphere had changed, for Bastian was allowed to inspect and admire all the ecclesiastical architecture he wished. He was also welcomed by university professors, some of whom were members of the Berlin Anthropological Society, of which Bastian was one of the founders.

Since the railroad ended at Valparaiso, Bastian went on to Peru by steamer. His first glimpse of the great coastal desert, which runs from northern Chile to the northern boundary of Peru, was at Huasco, a tiny village made up of a few one-story adobe houses, the streets between them leading off into the arid, shadowless sand. Here and there a lonely mounted figure, dressed in the heavy Spanish riding clothes of the country, awaited the arrival of the steamer. A short railway went up to Copiapa, a mountain settlement in which there were copper mines operated by some Germans. Here Bastian saw his first Peruvian antiquities, woven belts, copper knives and clay pots. As the steamer proceeded up the coast, he became aware that all the settlements were located in river valleys (rivers fed by sierra lakes which run through the desert to the sea). Along the shores of the streams, oases existed in which there were plantations of sugar and cotton. The coastal peoples, whose villages were older than the Inca period (as early as 400–500 B.C.), specialized in weaving. Among the articles collected by Bastian were grinding stones for making tortillas, arrows, baskets and mummies wrapped in weavings and mats. At Arica, he was shown graves which had been thrown open by an earthquake. The ancient cemeteries were located in the desert where rain was absolutely unknown. The dead were buried in a crouching position, wrapped in layers and layers of textiles between whose folds small objects were placed. Other objects surrounded the mummies, the most important being pots in the form of fruit, vegetables, animals and people.

In Lima Bastian stayed at the Hotel Maury (which still

exists today). He was received by the German ambassador and met other foreign businessmen stationed there. Still in search of antiquities, he complained that prices had risen because the engineers, imported by Meiggs to build his railroad, had been buying them up for their local school museums. Most of what he got he picked up from private collectors. Archeology in Peru was rudimentary. The public museum collection was housed in the library of the College of San Carlos but their librarian had just died and no one seemed to know much about it.

Bastian visited the most important adobe and stone ruins on the coast near Lima. Paramonga, to the north, had stepped pyramids with traces of painted murals (they have since disappeared). Near Ancon, a beach resort, he dug up mummies swathed in textiles and then placed in baskets; the head was bent between the shoulders and the whole bundle surmounted by a false head, or mask. Here the eroded adobe mounds, made of thousands of oblong bricks, had stone foundations. At Pachacamac, to the south of Lima, there were ruined temples with traces of courtyards and some stone columns. In the time of the Incas, their dominant culture had been carried to the coast and mingled with that of the coastal people, which accounts for the mixture of adobe and stone in this site. Pachacamac was a ceremonial center for centuries and within its great mounds, which have never been properly excavated, many layers of ancient culture remain to be examined. Even today, the visitor sees fragments of skulls, textiles, and potsherds lying about, testimony to the efforts of treasure hunters, or *huaceros*, whose random plundering has done so much harm to the important sites of Peru. Bastian picked up some wooden figures and animal skulls.

The ethnologist's remarks concerning Lima reveal his sympathy with subject peoples. The Indians of the country were freed from actual slavery by President Castillo but "through the natural docility of the race many ways were found to keep them in some sort of servitude." Lima, he felt, covered with the false make-up of its public buildings in the French style was a corrupt pest hole. Its income was derived from mines worked by foreigners and sweated out of the Quechua Indians who, unable to live from their tiny patches of land (the lion's share of the country's acreage was in the hands of a few rich aristocrats) had to become part-time miners. After seeing the poverty-stricken, hardworking natives, Bastian "felt an intense anger toward the majority of the useless and lazy riff-raff of of the capital" who spent what came from the labors of the people in mad extravagance.

In addition, at this time, through misgovernment and the inroads of foreign entrepreneurs, such as the American Grace Line, Peru's currency had lost its value. It happened in the following way: foreign investors had lent large sums to the government (which it could not repay) in order to obtain the rights to export the products of Peru. The money from the loans was stolen or wasted by corrupt government officials. Thus, when it was known that the government was in debt and penniless, no one felt any confidence in the worth of the paper money it printed. This meant that manufactured goods from foreign countries cost immense amounts of Peruvian money and could not be bought by any one except the very rich. This caused real hardship because Peru itself had no industry and did not produce any factory-made articles.

Bastian had an interview with President Manuel Pardo who seemed concerned over the unhappy state of his country but appeared to be helpless. Bastian, always a missionary where it concerned anthropology and archeology, discussed these subjects with the president and found him at least interested in science.

The ethnologist's next objective was Ecuador; from Callao to Guayaquil in Ecuador he again travelled by ship. Around

Guayaquil he obtained some antiquities, mostly stone or clay images. He heard of a stone figure of an ape, set up by the Indians in a village plaza and apparently worshipped. The trip to Quito, high in the mountains, was an arduous undertaking. (Today, scorning overland travel, the traveller flies up in a couple of hours.) Bastian was able to take a small steamer up the Guayaquil River which was infested with crocodiles, at that time often hunted for the skins which were sold in the United States. The next day from Gadua he set out with a mule for himself, one for his servant, a pack mule and a driver or *arriero*. The path, for there was no road, ran through a marshy area impassable in the rainy season. This area was, and still is, virgin jungle, difficult and dangerous to traverse because the mule might sink to its knees or stumble over roots. Branches lashed the traveller, he had to be on guard against becoming entangled in low-hanging lianas and dragged off his saddle. "As the dark, grim forest and underbrush grew thinner, through a clearing a wooded mountain top could be seen wreathed in mist. After many windings of the river had been crossed, the road began to climb a ravine, revealing vistas below, where the river roared, and above varied glimpses of green, shadowy woods and light on the changing pattern of the hills that shut in the valley. Here and there were small sugar plantations strewn with straw huts. Guarape [juice of sugar cane] was a refreshing drink. A custom encountered throughout the country was to use brown raw sugar (panelo or chaucara) as a snack with a drink of water."

The road zigzagged higher and higher up into the mountains until the party reached a real highway, paved with cobblestones. From here there was a panoramic view and in the distance, looking back toward the coast, clouds, mountains and sea blended into one another. Eight-thousand-four-hundred-fifty feet up, Bastian arrived at a small town with a note of introduction to one of the residents. Bastian sent the note to the man by his servant and settled down to relax from weary hours in the saddle. Much to his astonishment, a stream of townspeople whom he had never heard of arrived to pay ceremonial visits. He later learned that the recipient of the letter had announced his arrival throughout the hamlet by means of the town crier. As a result he became either a VIP or a curiosity, he was not sure which. In such small sierra villages, a foreigner was practically a being from another world.

In Quito, a charming red-roofed city, whose streets wander up the side of a high valley and whose churches are the finest examples of colonial architecture in South America, he set about searching for antiquities. Although he made friends with the German merchants and the English and American ambassadors, few had bothered to buy any antiquities and the owner of the only local collection was away. He was told that stones, with the sun and the moon carved upon them, had been built into the foundations of a monastery and subsequently removed to the College of the Jesuits. Since then they had been broken. He urged that a search be made but nothing turned up. There was no public museum of archeology (there is still none) and practically nothing had been done in the way of excavation in this former northern kingdom of the Incas. Outside of Quito he found a small hollow mound, within it some stonework and traces of supporting beams, Most of the Inca stonework of the area had been obliterated when the building blocks were removed to be used in Spanish churches.

He admired the paintings of Miguel de Santiago and the painted wooden sculpture of Bernardo Legardo, the best known artists of the Quito school, for Quito was acknowledged as the center of artistic culture in the colonial period. Bastian also noted the Jívaro Indians from the interior were selling shrunken heads in the capital.

When Bastian met the Ecuadorian president Garcia Moreno,

he described him as a "deeply committed personality." Discussing his favorite subjects with him, the ethnologist was delighted to hear that the ruler of Ecuador intended to found a museum of archeology and anthropology in the near future. They talked about using systems of classification and display which Bastian had worked out in Berlin. These hopes were to be dashed by a national tragedy which took place the following day. Garcia was shot down in the presidential palace by three assassins, only one of whom was immediately caught.

The country was in an uproar. The streets of the capital were full of panic-stricken crowds running hither and thither. Merchants closed their shops and barricaded their houses. The streets were full of soldiers who did not know who was friend and who enemy. There were rumors of revolution. Garcia Moreno had been a complete dictator, he had never delegated authority and now the government was headless with no one prepared to take over. Bastian saw the corpse laid out in the cathedral surrounded by doctors whose services were useless. Not all the populace wept for the dead president. He had come to power through bloodshed. Unlike many South American dictators, however, he had the reputation of being financially honest. When Bastian heard there was talk of a revolutionary pronouncement in Guayaquil, he decided it was time for him to leave.

It was not so easy to leave during a revolution. Special exit permission was needed and there was a scarcity of horses because the army was requisitioning them. The governor of the state helped with the exit visa and the horses. But then the anthropologist was subjected to a process which is familiar to anyone who has traveled in South America; he had to go from government office to government office to obtain permissions which were granted, then countermanded and then granted again. He noted, however, that during South American revolutions the rights of foreigners were generally respected. Bastian ran into a streak of luck for he was able to purchase a whole collection of antiquities which had been assembled for display in the World's Exposition at Philadelphia but which no one had gotten around to sending there.

Bastian and his servant boarded a small sailboat headed down the Guayaquil River for the port. He noted immediately that ten times as many passengers as the boat could properly accommodate got on, among them a large contingent of uncombed, unwashed Indians plus a hundred sheep. In order to move from stem to stern of the boat, it was necessary to climb over their backs. At the first curve of the river, the boat went aground on a sandbank. When this mishap was overcome, the female passengers began to get seasick. In the close quarters aboard the miserable craft this was highly distressing. Then Bastian's loyal servant came to tell him that the boat was full of water and would soon sink.

In no time at all the news spread all over the boat. Amid a chorus of screams for help, the captain calmly went off in a canoe, supposedly to get help. The inexpert crew did nothing; the passengers wailed and howled and finally began to sing parts of the church litany. Bastian succeeded in organizing some of the young women, who were more stalwart than the men, to start bailing. Then he nagged and threatened one of the crew into taking the helm and steering for shore. Fortunately, at this point the wind strengthened and the boat made some headway. Bastian had with him a chest of seventy bronze axes which he had located and bought in the sierras. Some of the passengers wanted them thrown overboard to lighten the boat. The anthropologist was in favor of throwing the sheep overboard and allowing them to swim. When his opponents grew hysterical, Bastian stood over his precious axes with a loaded pistol. At last, when his female bailers began to give out, he threw water over the church choir. This brought them to their senses. They apologized for their behavior. "We

are animals!" they said. He was able to persuade them to bail.
The boat had now reached the mouth of the river and sailed
through a forest, the trunks of the trees partly under water.
By midnight, the water had been bailed low enough so that
the leak was found and repaired with melted lead. The next
morning, when they had safely docked, the captain turned up
as if nothing had happened. Bastian's irrepressible servant, who
was wearing a picture of the Virgin of Quinche, explained
that it was thanks to her aid that he had noticed the leak and
saved them all.

At Guayaquil once more, Bastian took the steamer, *Are-
quipa*, down to Payta, for he wished to visit northern Peru.
At Piura, the tropical coast came to an end and Sechura
desert began. This had to be crossed by mules or horses and
it was a particularly dangerous journey because the area was
infested with *zambo* bandits. Zambo was the Peruvian word
for a person who was part Negro in addition to being part
Indian. Negroes had been imported into Peru to work on the
sugar plantations of the north.

The horses' feet at times sank deeply into the greyish sand
unbroken by any tree under the blue-grey sky. Here and
there could be seen the whitened bones of some animal which
had strayed into the desert and perished for lack of water.
Crosses were also set up along the route to show where travellers had been murdered by bandits. All this was not an
encouraging sight.

They reached a small settlement called Motufe, where
Bastian hoped to get some much needed rest, but after an
hour and a half of sleep, the guide woke him again. Since a
caravan was just starting out, they would be safer riding with
it for there was talk of bandits. Aware of the perennially unsettled state of Peru, Bastian pulled himself together and once
more got into the saddle. "The sandy character of the road
continued, but the landscape was now covered with bushes

and, on the side toward the sea, the plane ended, changing
into hilly projections of the cape. In the distance, signs of the
town of Lambayeque appeared when suddenly, from the side
of the road two shots rang out. The caravan was thrown into
great confusion, the better mounted rushed off at full gallop
toward the city, doubtless with the intention of getting help,
to put the best construction on it, the others with mules, pack
animals, women and children, crowded together and did not
know whether to go backwards or forwards. A couple of
muleteers stood their ground for better or for worse, as they
happened to be armed and thereupon my guide got his double-
barreled gun ready. On my side there was a couple of revolver
shots, then the bandits decided, when at close range they discovered they had to do with foreigners and could make out
the weapons, that they had better leave the train unmolested
and, after circling a couple of times, disappeared into the
bushes from whence they had sprung."

It was all in the day's work. At Lambayeque, he was once
more examining cemeteries and noted that panpipes, made of
clay, which he found in graves, still existed in bamboo, and
were played by Indian musicians (they still are today).

The last important ruin which he visited was Chanchan, a
coastal metropolis of stone and adobe. It was a walled city
with reservoirs, temples and blocks of houses arranged in
gridiron patterns. Some of the houses still had traces of straw
roofs. (Excavations in the 1940s revealed murals in reliefs
and in color.) Most significant was that from Chanchan, and
from pyramid temples of the sun and moon nearby, countless
objects had been recovered. Two cultures, now called the
Mochica and a later phase, the Chimu, were represented.
Bastian had an interview with a leading *huacero* and once
more was in despair to hear of the melting down of gold and
silver treasures. The ceramic grave pots, or *huacos*, were of
special interest because, in this region, they were made in every

conceivable shape. Fish, birds, animals, vegetables, warriors, kings and commoners appeared either molded in three dimensions or painted in little friezes that were reminiscent of early Greek vases. Here, grave pots were a vivid historical record without words. Alas, anything that was not gold or silver the huacero had given away. Bastian pressed him to recover them and together they visited the man's friends. Nothing remained, all had been broken, given to children as toys, thoughtlessly tossed away. The *huacero* remembered he had sent a few pots to other friends in Lima. Later, Bastian actually recovered some of them from a rubbish heap. Bastian tried to teach the treasure-hunter the value of all ancient objects and urged him to get in touch with museums when he found others. The situation was typical of the early days of archeology for even Bastian thought chiefly of amassing material for his museum. Neither he nor anyone else was in a position to excavate carefully, noting the position, relationship between, and distribution of objects, particularly pieces of pottery, which were eventually, when methods were better, to yield information which would make it possible to describe and date early cultures.

When Bastian left Peru, he moved on to Colombia by sea for he was anxious to obtain Chibcha material which his museum lacked. The Chibchas were a group which up to the coming of the Spaniards had lived in the Valley of the Magdalena River. They were notable for their fine craftmanship in gold. The style of their jewelry differed from that of the Quechuas in Peru. They were ruled by a priest-king, a functionary interesting to Bastian as another example of "elementary ideas." From his own observation and studies he felt that here was an institution similar to that found in Africa, Polynesia and Asia, particularly Japan. At the same time he commented on the difference in temperament between the melancholy South American mountain people and the gay

Africans and Japanese. This was an example of similar levels
of culture producing similar institutions with local modifica-
tions. It was perhaps the cold, difficult climate which affected
the character of the mountain Indians. After Bastian lectured
in Bogota, local scholars presented him with a priceless collection of antiquities.

The rest of the German anthropologist's trip included stops
at Veraguas (Panama), Costa Rica and Guatemala. He was
disappointed to find the territory was so wild that he could
not travel overland. Only in Guatemala did he spend some
time. He met the director of the museum in Guatemala City,
was shown old heiroglyphic manuscripts of the Maya and saw
something of their carved stone monuments and temples, concerning which he was to publish a book.

The return journey took him across the United States, his
most important stop being at Washington to visit the Smithsonian Institution (already a thriving ethnological institution)
and meet its director. He returned to Berlin by way of a
steamer from New York, having traveled for a year and a half.

Bastian took time to found the German *Ethnological Review* and the Society for Anthropology, Ethnology and Prehistory, to be president of the Geological Society, and to teach
at the University of Berlin. In 1880, he went to the South Seas
but of this trip he has left us no account. He was chiefly interested in mythology and stories of the origin and development
of the world which he recorded in five volumes which appeared in the next five years. He lamented that wherever
he went, he saw ruins not only of material achievements but
also of simple but colorful ways of life. Of the Polynesians
he said, "The moment they become acquainted with us, the
angel of death comes to them." It is the constant complaint
of every dedicated anthropologist.

In 1886, a new ethnological building opened with Bastian
as its director. The collections in the old Imperial Museum

had occupied a couple of badly lighted rooms in the rear building. They were arranged geographically, but tribes and peoples were not identified. Bastian filled the whole first floor of the new museum with carefully documented exhibits, a large part of which he himself had collected. He built it into one of the best institutions of its kind in the world, rivaling the Pitt Rivers Museum at Oxford and the Smithsonian at Washington.

Bastian's ideas concerning the colonial problem reflected the ambitions of his own country. England had a monopoly in the Orient, which it had sealed off with its great navy, but Germany could be a friendly rival in Africa. Despite what he had seen of the seamy side of colonialism and the remark quoted about the Polynesians, he was a man of his time. He accepted the gospel that Europe's culture was superior and that Europe had a historic mission to spread it all over the less developed world, at the same time linking the globe in a widespread network of commerce and industry. Such a doctrine, which has been shown up as a failure in the last fifty years, did not take into account that so-called backward peoples have their pride and their individuality and would not be content to be docile pupils of the condescending white man.

Continuing his field trips, Bastian ranged through Turkestan, India, Java and Bali. In the nineties he came back from Malaysia a living corpse but his iron constitution pulled him through. In his seventy-seventh year, in 1903, he set off with a German writer, Berthold Mehrer, on his ninth journey, which was to include Malaysia, Jamaica and Trinidad. The flesh at last failed the indomitable spirit in Port of Spain, Trinidad. After six days of illness, he died there. There was only his friend Mehrer to accompany him to the grave, sitting on the mule-drawn wagon that carried the coffin. The German consul turned up late, apologizing for having missed the lonely ceremony.

Bastian's central concept of elementary ideas stated that these ideas seemed to arise spontaneously everywhere; they could be borrowed and modified but they were limited, they were in fact "of an appalling monotony." The invention of the fire-drill, stone scrapers and axes, to mention material creations, forms such as exogamy (the custom that a man must marry a woman from a different tribe), the concept of personified nature or of the soul, these basic human achievements were universal. Efforts have sometimes been made to relate elementary ideas to the "collective unconscious," elaborated by the psychoanalyst Carl Jung. They are distinctly different. Jung put forward the unscientific, and generally unacceptable notion that characteristics or skills or concepts developed by an individual could somehow be inherited physically by later generations. This mystical concept does not appeal to most anthropologists who do not see how ideas can be transmitted through the cells of the body but feel that culture is passed on through the learning process.

According to Bastian, a people who lived by the water, for instance, would automatically think of the fishhook and the fishnet. Each geographical area therefore produced a specific emotional and intellectual character in the inhabitants; they were shaped by their environment. Thus, what the anthropologist calls "culture areas" would be modified by contacts with other culture areas, and one would need to study diffusion through the movements of peoples, trading, and wars in order to understand the behavior of a particular group of people.

In Bastian's view, civilization was a product of an infinite number of mixtures, exchanges and blendings, some of the results worked well, others died out. It was a theory which paralleled Darwin's account of the physical survival of certain species through their better adaptation to their environment yet, curiously enough, Bastian was obstinately anti-Darwin.

Bastian's ideas, when he does not obscure them with over-complicated and disorganized writing, are advanced for his period. He neither tried to classify individual traits and pin them down as museum directors tended to do, nor did he try to oversimplify human society in terms of one simple line of development from lower to higher forms. His theory of an interplay between basic human psychological reactions and the necessities of the environment is as valid today as in his time.

As a man, he impresses us as tremendously solid. To traverse the world, as he did, he must have had a great appetite for life and he certainly never spared his tough, resistant body. He was evidently quite fearless, as various episodes we have narrated show. At the same time, the ability to relax and get drunk with an African prince indicates that he was neither unsociable nor a European snob. A certain dry humor enabled him to deal with peoples who lacked European habits of industry, efficiency and reliability. Somewhat narrow, lacking any interest in the arts, his firmness of purpose never slackened. He seems always to have known just what he wanted and to have in most cases succeeded in getting it. Yet, there is a hint of the poet in his contemplation of the unity of mankind, and his sensitive descriptions of scenery show that he responded to the beauty of the natural world. One side of his character remains a mystery. If he was ever involved with women, this part of his life was carefully censored. He had evidently many warm professional friendships with men and casual contacts he managed with ease, but only a man with no home life, with no strong personal tie, would have spent so much of his time away from his own country. Was there something lacking, was his restless roaming of the earth a search for something he never found? His lonely death somehow suggests a touch of melancholy and unfulfillment in a life busy with scientific activity and objective achievement.

# BRONISLAW MALINOWSKI

In 1914, the anthropological section of the British Association for the Advance of Science met in Melbourne, Australia. No sooner had the scientists gathered than World War I broke out. It was an embarrassing situation for the German and Austrian scholars, who were put in the position of enemy aliens. Some of them were interned for the duration of the war but, at the same time, given complete freedom to continue working. A young Pole who happened to be an Austrian subject because he came from the city of Cracow (then a part of the Austrian Empire) was among those trapped in Australia. For him it was no hardship because he had already prepared to carry out his research in the South Seas.

Bronislaw Malinowski was born in 1844 in Cracow. His father was of the nobility, a landowner and also a professor of Slavic Philology. The elder Malinowski died when Bronislaw was only a boy and, as a result, he grew up very close to his mother. Indeed, at one point when he was unable to read because of an eye operation, she read anthropology treatises aloud to him. Judging from the evidence of his diaries, he was a highly emotional, neurotic young man. In the university sphere he soon displayed intellectual ability, obtaining a degree in physics and mathematics in 1908. Apparently the threat of tuberculosis forced him to temporarily discontinue his studies. He tells us that he walked out of the library of the University of Cracow with the three green volumes of Sir James Frazer's *Golden Bough* under his arm. To occupy his enforced leisure, he decided to read this pioneer work in anthropology in English. "No sooner had I read this great work than I became immersed in it and enslaved by it. I realized then that anthropology, as presented by Sir James Frazer, is a great science, worthy of as much devotion as any of her elder and more exact sister studies and I became bound to the service of Frazerian anthropology."

He does not seem to have immediately acted upon this enthusiasm because he worked in Leipzig under the experimental psychologist, Wilhelm Wundt, and did not arrive in England until 1910. Wundt taught a brand of psychology which involved measuring the reactions of the senses to stimuli. Among his experiments was twirling discs, colored in different ways, in order to determine the perceptions of the receiving mechanism of the eyes. It was a limited area of investigation but it was objective. All through his later career, Malinowski showed an interest in psychology which was perhaps awakened by his apprenticeship to Wundt.

When Malinowski came to England, he studied in the London School of Economics where he met and made friends with Frazer and trained in anthropology under A. C. Haddon and C. G. Seligman. Haddon had done important field work in the Torres Strait, north of New Guinea. Seligman had participated in the same expedition, specializing in native medicine. It was Seligman to whom Malinowski was particularly indebted for encouragement and practical help in his career. The older scholar was so impressed by his talents that when there was an opening on the staff, Seligman offered to take a cut in his own salary in order to make it possible to hire his brilliant student.

Malinowski's first book was a study of the family among the aborigines of Australia, published in 1913. In the same year, he was appointed to a lectureship in the London school. When, in 1914, he was interned by the Australian authorities, Seligman used his influence to get him a scholarship financed by Robert Mond, a prominent British industrialist. The young scholar's friends in England carried so much weight with the Australian authorities that even they were induced to contribute to his work in the South Seas.

On the twelfth of September, he arrived at Port Moresby, New Guinea. Distant mountains were covered with morning mist. Rocky cliffs bordered the sea. Offshore, there was a coral reef with portions of the wreck of a steam yacht stranded on it. The wind was cold and the anthropologist felt washed-out and dull for he had been very seasick on the trip. Port Moresby was "the kind of a place you hear a lot about and expect a good deal of, but that turns out to be utterly different." There was a deep circular bay reflecting a calm blue sky. On one side, a cone-shaped hill stood at the entrance to another inlet which extended into deep twin bays further inland. The beach was covered with pebbles and skimpy dried grass and littered with refuse. Along it ran a broad path which passed a wireless station, crossed a narrow beach with a few mangroves and led to native villages.

Malinowski was entertained by the governor and found the Australian government officials dull. He immediately set about gathering information from the Melanesians. The old men who came together "squatted in a row along the wall of a hut, fuzzy heads on dark torsos, dressed in torn old shirts, patched-up jaegers and pieces of khaki uniform while under

these civilized clothes peeped out *sihis*, a kind of belt which
covers the thighs and adjacent parts of the body. The bamboo
pipe circulated rapidly. A little intimidated by this conclave,
I sat down at the table and opened a book."

After spending the day asking questions about family relationships and ancestry, he felt more like an anthropologist:

> I felt not too distinctly or strongly but surely that a bond was
> growing up between myself and this landscape. The calm bay
> was framed in the curving branches of a mangrove tree, which
> were also reflected in the mirror of the water and on the damp
> beach. The purple glow in the west penetrated the palm grove
> and covered the scorched grass with its blaze, slithering over
> the dark sapphire waters—everything was pervaded with a
> promise of fruitful work and unexpected success; it seemed a
> paradise in comparison with the monstrous hell I had expected.

This was only a mood, however. In all of the pages of the
diary he kept, covering most of the time spent in the New
Guinea and Trobriand area, Malinowski is prey to the most
violently conflicting moods. At least half of his days are spent
in boredom and depression. The nervous, introspective, over-
sensitive Pole found it very hard to convince himself that he
was getting anywhere. His field work was a pioneer effort for
he was not in sympathy with the two prevailing trends in his
field. One, called diffusionism, consisted in putting together
evidence of the spread of customs, artifacts, ideas, myths which
were found simultaneously in different places. These culture
complexes, as they were named, were supposed to indicate the
movement of peoples and the development and spread of cultures. Taken together with the idea of gradual evolution from
lower to higher forms, various theories about human society
had been constructed. The other trend was the preoccupation
with the past history of man, a continual attempt to trace the

evolution of culture before the time of written records. All of this Malinowski considered too ambitious, based largely on the imagination of the scholars, and impractical. Thanks to his training in such precise sciences as physics and mathematics, he wanted to bring anthropology down to earth, to make it factual. As yet, however, he did not know in what direction he wanted to go. He discovered almost immediately that most missionaries, traders and officials knew nothing about Melanesians; they regarded them as little above brute animals. Yet, he himself was not sure how to penetrate to the realities of island life. He was reduced to asking rather desultory questions. The dark, wrinkled faces were enigmatic, sometimes they seemed wilfully hostile. What did he have in common with them? Did they have any secrets worth discovering? Above all, he did not know their language.

There was little to be learned at Port Moresby where the Melanesians, thanks to contacts with the Europeans, were losing their own way of life. Malinowski did observe, however, a native method of hunting in which fires were lit to drive the game to the hunters:

Fires had been kindled in a few places. Marvelous spectacle. Red, sometimes purple flames crawled up the hillside in narrow ribbons; through the dark blue or sapphire smoke the hillside changes color like a black opal under the glint of its polished surface. From the hillside in front of us the fire went on down into the valley, eating at the tall grasses. Roaring like a hurricane of light and heat, it came straight toward us, the wind behind it whipping half burnt bits into the air. Birds and crickets fly past in clouds. I walked right into the flames. Marvelous—some completely mad catastrophe rushing straight at me with furious speed.

Malinowski moved to Mailu, an island off the southeast coast of New Guinea. Here again, after a first mood of delight and optimism, after a few days, he was bored and, instead of escaping by getting drunk, Malinowski took to reading novels. For him they became a kind of tranquilizer to quiet his nerves and to prevent him from doing what he knew he should do. At this point his opiates were Thackeray's *Vanity Fair* and Conrad's *Romance*. He wrote:

> I had a feeling of joy, freedom, happiness. Yet only a few days of it and I was escaping from it to the company of Thackeray's London snobs, following them eagerly around the streets of that big city. I longed to be in Hyde Park in Bloomsbury—I even enjoyed the advertisement in the London newspapers. I am incapable of burying myself in my work, of accepting voluntary captivity and making the most of it.

At the same time, he suffered from various imaginary illnesses. During all of this period of field work, he continuously worried about his heart, complained of nervous spells, had insomnia, dosed himself with (evidently unnecessary) cathartics and then complained about diarrhea. In addition, he was continually feeding himself arsenic which he seemed to consider a sort of tonic.

The missionary on Mailu, a certain W. J. Saville, who was later to write about New Guinea, seems to have been a continual irritant. Malinowski was disgusted by the attitude of white superiority which Saville adopted toward the natives. In addition, he thought him stupid, poorly educated and insensitive. Since the anthropologist took his meals at the Reverend Saville's house, he had plenty of opportunities to be rubbed the wrong way. In addition to moodiness of character, the Polish scholar never really forgot his aristocratic background. It was revealed in a certain lordly arrogance in dealings with people. Even a visit from his former teacher, Haddon, did not seem to make him happier. "Passions and moods: hatred for Haddon for annoying me, for conspiring with the missionary." This time he took to Dumas's *The Count of Monte Cristo*.

Despite his professional difficulties, Malinowski was capable of enjoying the sea and the water. A trip on a sailing raft emphasized the excitement of the tropics.

> Under a yellow sail spreading its wings. . . . I felt that one is strong on the waves—on such a raft—direct contact with the sea. On the green water—turquoise, only transparent—the violet silhouettes of the mountains, like shadows cast on the screen of the fog. Behind me over the trees of the jungle, covering the shore, slopes a lofty pyramid covered with woods. In front of me a glittering belt of yellow sand, above it the silhouettes of palm trees seem to grow up out of the sea. A coral island. The water laps between the boards of the raft—the sea peeps through the holes and the spray smashing along the edges of the boat. A sandbank and the boys push the boat off. The bottom is visible —purple weeds in the transparent green. Mailu in the distance— the mist-colored silhouette of volcanic rock with a noble profile. A little village—with a few well-built houses of the Mailu type and several characteristic tumble-down huts. A few trees on the bare sand—for the rest, little grey houses; dark columns protrude from waves of yellow sand. Surrounded with a fence—in spite of that—pigs walk about as they like among the houses.

To escape from the missionary, Malinowski consorted with the ne'er-do-well son of a Protestant Irish lord, Richard de Moleyns, otherwise known as Dirty Dick. Dick was not well educated and drank like a fish but at least offered a different kind of campanionship. Life in his unwalled hut, which consisted of verandas separated by screens, was relaxed and sloppy. Dick, himself, unshaven, wearing pajamas all day like the traditional beachcomber, lived in filth but surrounded by numerous servants. Malinowski's lack of religious faith may have had something to do with his dislike of the missionary. The story is told that when an old Jew in a railroad train once asked him why he believed, the Polish scholar thought it over, decided that he had no basis for belief, gave up religious observance and became an agnostic. His final judgment of missionaries like Saville was that they persecuted natives who were not friendly to the mission. The sum total of their efforts was to destroy the Melanesian joy of life, to destroy their psychological reason for existence. They struggled ruthlessly against local tradition and continually created new needs among the preliterates. "No question but they do harm."

Although much of his time was spent squabbling with the missionary over the use of a small boat, making up the quarrels, and occasionally working over Saville's notes, or lying nervously exhausted in his tent, he continued to force himself to question various informants to make some progress in learning the local language, Motu. Now and then he made excursions to other islands and on one of them, Loupom, the inhabitants were making ready for a feast. Here the palm-thatched houses were tall and magnificent with effigies of totemic animals carved on the boards over the entrances. In the evening, he tells us: "For the first time I heard the protracted, piercing sound of a sea shell being blown—kibi—and with it a monstrous squealing of pigs and roar of men. In the silence of the night, it gave the impression of some mysterious atrocity being perpetrated and threw a sudden light—a somber light—on forgotten cannibal ceremonies." The next day the people wore holiday clothes, some of the women had bones through their noses, the men had on necklaces made of shell circles and they carried ebony sticks in their hands. Those in mourning had been painted and shone "like chimney sweeps."

Malinowski finally paid to have a woman's dance performed. The women wore feathers on their heads and, when pigs were brought in to be prepared for the feast, danced to meet them to the sound of drums.

Perhaps the most striking institution which Malinowski recorded was that of head-hunting, a custom widely practiced in New Guinea and the South Seas in the past and even to this day being carried on by some of the tribes not in contact with western administrators. The Mailu killed (by stealth) a man, woman or child, left the body and brought the head home. The amputation was done with a bamboo knife hung around the warrior's neck. The head was boiled in a pot which was then thrown into the sea. The skull, roughly cleaned, was smoked and dried to preserve it. While this went on, the village prepared a feast consisting of bananas, taro, sago and fish. When the skull was ready, a hole was drilled in it and it was hung in the men's house. This was celebrated by the feast and a dance in which the head-hunter carried the skull under his arm.

The taker of the head had to maintain tabus, eating no boiled food or fish for a certain period. If he violated the tabu, it was believed, his testicles would swell. As a result of his feat, he had the right to wear white cockatoo feathers at dances; those feathers were considered an emblem of his importance as a warrior. In general the taking of heads among preliterates seems to be equated with obtaining the strength and vitality of the person killed. Originally the victim would have been a warrior but the substitution of women and children as victims would seem to indicate that the original meaning had become obscured.

Despite his efforts to gather information, Malinowski was still very much an outsider. He was undergoing a kind of apprenticeship, trying in vain to break down the barrier of his European culture. His built-in feeling of superiority was complicated by his lordly sense of an aristocratic background. At moments of low ebb, his feelings were pure hostility. "I was furious at them, particularly because after I gave them their portions of tobacco they all went away. On the whole my feelings toward the natives are decidely tending to *Exterminate the brutes.*"

The turning point in Malinowski's career came after a brief return to Melbourne. He decided to do field work among the Trobriand Islanders. In 1915, he sailed past the southern coast of New Guinea on his way to this new area of investigation. Visible from the ship were steep folded slopes covered with dense, rank jungle, spotted here and there with brighter patches of grass. The intense green contrasted with the azure of the sea and the sharp bright beach. The mountains faded off into steamy tropical mists. Plastered on the slopes were big triangular clearings whose apexes pointed uphill. Villages were hidden on the foreshore in groves of trees through which here and there the glinting gold and purple of palm thatch could be seen. The ship had circled the end of the great island of New Guinea. It sailed into the lagoon of Boyowa, the main island of the Trobriands, which was to be the anthropologist's base for several years. The sea became greenish, broken only by sandbanks. Some of these were bare, some were clothed in a few pandanus trees, their roots high in the sand. There were intricate passages into the lagoon where the tangled matting of the jungle broke over the beaches. In vistas through the foliage palm groves could be seen, the trunks seeming to support the green roof-like pillars. A closer view revealed a less romantic scene. Canoes were drawn high up on the beach which was covered with mud and refuse, coconut shells, dead crabs, half-buried shells. When the launch, which had brought the anthropologist to shore from the ship, moved away, Malinowski was left on the beach overcome by one of his familiar moods of depression. He made his way to the house of a trader and pearl buyer who took him into his compound.

On his first visits to the village with the white trader, some of the natives flocked around him begging for tobacco, always his stock in trade when he had to buy their services. The older and more dignified remained seated before the high-arching housefronts. He made visits to the village by himself and tried in pidgin English to collect terms of kinship and family histories. Once again, language was a barrier. Information seemed mangled and unintelligible. He felt that he had reached a dead end. He tried to pump the traders but found that even though they had lived in the tropics for years their lack of interest in natives made their information almost useless.

He reacted in his usual way by reading novels to forget his troubles. It is something of a mystery where he got so many books, unless he arrived with a well-stocked library. All during his Trobriand field work, he records that he was still reading for escape, making good resolutions to break the habit only to fall back into the arms of Kipling, Hardy, Conrad, sometimes even taking refuge in the work of trivial popular novelists who are now forgotten.

At length he made a drastic decision. He put up his tent in the middle of the native village and endeavored to cut himself off from white men entirely. Although this was not the first time an anthropologist had done this (Franz Boas had lived with the Eskimos a couple of decades before), Malinowski made it part of his anthropological platform and it was because of this that it has become standard procedure since for a field worker to obtain his doctorate by an apprenticeship spent living with a native group. Indeed, in the case of Malinowski, it was for his publication on the natives of Mailu that he received a doctorate from the University of London in 1916.

Each morning he walked through the village, watching the islanders cooking, joking among themselves, playing with their children, sometimes quarreling, working at their handicrafts or fishing in the lagoon.

The Trobrianders were Melanesians, an ethnic group distinct from the fairer-skinned Polynesians. Their ancestors had probably in ages past come from Asia where originally a mixture of strains, including some Mongoloid and rather more Australoid, had produced a strong well-built people varying from dark brown to a lighter coffee color. Their hair was sometimes long and frizzed out, sometimes close-cropped. The men wore a palm leaf G-string, the women palm leaf skirts.

The village lay on a fertile level plain surrounded by low scrub broken by gardens. Vines trained on long poles looked like an exuberant patch of pole beans. Around the village was a grove of coconut palms. Two concentric rings of huts with a street passing between them circled a dancing ground and the chief's hut and yam house. The inner circle of huts were also yam houses. The huts were built of poles with tall thatches shaped like gothic arches, the sides walled with woven mats. The yam houses were more impressive than the dwellings for much of the ceremonial life had to do with this vegetable. The chief's hut had a gable end, carved and painted with red, black and white decorations.

Malinowski's villagers grew so accustomed to his presence that they ceased to be self-conscious. He poked his nose into everything and they soon regarded him "as part and parcel of their life, a necessary evil or nuisance."

As he learned their language, he also learned good manners and discretion and thus was able to share in their occupations, their amusements and their ceremonials. Rites, births, deaths took place while he watched. Anything dramatic that happened he was able to investigate while the villagers were suffi-

ciently interested to talk about it. Thus he captured their
emotional attitudes and real opinions first hand.

The most dramatic occurrence, which he describes in detail,
was a falling out between the chief and his heirs. Among the
Trobrianders, inheritance was through the female line, which
meant that a chief was succeeded by his sister's son. He was,
however, emotionally attached to his own favorite son, Namwana Guya'u. Namwana Guya'u accused his rival and cousin,
Mitakata, of misbehavior with his wife. He even went so far
as to bring Mitakata up before the white magistrate and get
him imprisoned for a month or so. The chief shut himself up
in his hut when this happened for Mitakata's kinsmen were
boiling with rage. By nightfall, the villagers had just settled
down to a very subdued supper, leaving the central plaza
empty, when suddenly a loud voice rang through the village.
The eldest brother of the imprisoned man stood before his hut
and addressed the invisible Guya'u.

"Namwana Guya'u, you are a cause of trouble. We, the
Tabalu of Omarakana, allowed you to stay here, to live among
us. You ate our food. You partook of the flesh of pigs brought
to us as a tribute. You sailed in our canoe. You built a hut
on our soil. Now you have done us harm. You have told lies.
Mitakata is in prison. We refuse to let you stay here. This is
our village! You are a stranger here. Go away! We drive you
away! We drive you out of Omarakana!"

All this was shouted in a loud piercing voice trembling with
emotion. Each sentence, spoken after a pause, was hurled like
a missile across the empty space at the hut inside of which
the accused sat ashamed and brooding. After this, the younger
sister of Mitakata rose and spoke and then one of his younger
brothers. Their words were almost the same, each being the
formula of expulsion from the village.

The speeches were received in the deepest silence. Nobody

stirred. Before the night was over, however, Namwana Guya'u had left the village forever. He moved a few miles away to the village from which his mother originally came. The chief remained in his hut for several days and when he came out looked aged and broken by grief. His sympathies were with his favorite son but the law of custom was on the side of the heirs. No power could change the decree of exile. A man who tried to go against such a tradition would be dishonored. No Trobriander would think of attempting such a defiance.

Yet there was emotional rebellion. The old chief would not speak to Mitakata's kinsmen. For a year or two, none of them were taken with him on trading expeditions, a privilege to which they were entitled. Two years later, when the anthropologist returned to the island, Namwana Guya'u was still in the other village although he sometimes visited Omarakana to be with his father. His mother, however, had suffered emotional shock at his expulsion. The natives said, "She wailed and wailed and refused to eat and died." And Mitakata himself repudiated his wife because she was of the same clan as his enemy, Namwana Guya'u.

An incident such as this told Malinowski much about several institutions. In the first place, the conflicts of loyalty caused by inheritance through the female line were clearly dramatized. The role of the father was an emotional one toward his off-spring but without real authority because the family leadership lay with his sisters, their husbands and the latter's sons.

The rite of expulsion was typical of the method by which justice was administered in their group. There was no police or judicial system. Social approval or disapproval was what mattered. If any member of the village behaved badly, was stingy or unjust, the whole village talked about it and condemned him. If the crime was serious, the casting-out ritual was used by the injured parties. Shame was the emotion which brought about punishment. A man, returning from fishing, found his wife in bed with a chief from a nearby village. Public opinion was against the chief. Out of shame he took fish poison, a kind of halfway suicide, for the poison was not really deadly. He was given emetics, recovered, and eventually regained his prestige.

Actual suicide did take place. The younger wife of a chief was suspected by her elder and less attractive co-wife, who spied on her and caught her deceiving her husband. The guilty wife was publicly attacked by the relatives of her husband. Her sense of shame was profound. She dressed in her best, climbed a palm tree, wailed aloud and jumped from it. The need for status and prestige and the sense of obligation to perform traditional tasks and actions was enough to keep most individuals well-behaved in a small preliterate society on a coral island.

Above all, such incidents as this showed very clearly how important the family was in the social structure of the group and how tightly blood and marriage relationships bound every member of the group in a web of duties and privileges.

By walking through the village on a fine morning Malinowski could see much of the routine of coral island life. Each family, man, wife and children would be eating a quick breakfast, mostly leftovers from last night's meal. (Polygamy was practiced only by wealthy men of high rank.) Then the bigger children would help lay out the work implements for the day. The women used a bell-shaped basket to collect shellfish or wild fruits. This they had to carry on their heads on a pad while men were permitted to carry loads only on their shoulders. The women also were in charge of coconut water bottles which they sometimes carried a half mile to a waterhole. This was a kind of club and center of gossip as they filled the bottles, stoppered them with a twist of palm leaves and put them in baskets.

The men would be off to their occupations of getting timber, using a stone or metal adze and axe, canoe building, gardening, hunting, or fishing with nets and fishhooks. The men had exclusive possession of spears, drums, dancing ornaments and shell necklaces and armlets used in trading.

At night, the family would be back, the women preparing a meal of yams and fish or pork. The men often took care of the babies, for in this particular society a father did not consider it beneath him to wash and feed the infant, often carrying his child about with him for hours.

Heavier jobs such as clearing the ground for gardens or building houses were the province of the men as were trading trips by canoe. Women, however, looked after the pigs and weeded the gardens. Men did the woodcarving and made their own belts and pubic leaves. Women were exclusively involved with the manufacture of their own brilliant dancing costumes. Red and purple dyes were mixed in huge clamshells, then banana and pandanus leaves were steeped in the color and hung up to dry, thus adding a note of gaiety to the village.

Although the husband was supposed to be master of the household, he had no control over his wife's property and her hereditary rights gave her a certain importance. In cases of a domestic quarrel, Malinowski noted, anger was often expressed by the antagonists breaking each other's exclusive property. The man would smash the water bottles while the wife might attack his drum and dancing shield.

Malinowski had been planning to write Saville after the publication of his own article on Mailu. Saville, however, turned up in the Trobriands. There was embarrassment and exaggerated politeness on both sides. Malinowski, to mitigate his former conduct, accused himself of a persecution mania and pleaded bad health. Saville praised the article on Mailu "not very sincerely" and said he had helped all he could. The two even made plans for some future work in Mailu. Unfor-

tunately, by the next day, the old cat-and-dog relationship
began again. Saville made a tactless remark about Malinowski's wartime internment. Malinowski flared up. The anthropologist retired to sputter in his diary.

> I realized that Saville is a boor who must get on my nerves the
> moment he steps out of his shell and that I am incapable of
> treating him as a means pure and simple. . . . As a personality
> he is repulsive and contemptible: a petty greengrocer blown up
> by his own sense of importance into a caricature of a petty
> sovereign.

In his relationship to Saville the contrast between his inner
feeling and his public behavior is intense. Against the quotation from his private diary just cited we can place his generous
introduction to Saville's own book (1926) which was not
without scholarly pretensions. Saville, it seems, had studied
his subject and had even attended Malinowski's own lectures
at the University of London in 1921. "The value of the book
consists to a large extent in the rare union of rich detail with
firm outline, of the full flavor of native life which we receive,
combined with a good grasp of the underlying scheme of
native organization." Malinowski could be generous toward
a rival even if the emotions of a prima donna fermented in
his soul.

Malinowski's personal life during his second residence in
the Trobriands was still complicated by moods of depression
and an involvement with two women. While in Melbourne,
he met Elsie R. Masson, daughter of Sir David Orme Masson,
professor of chemistry at the University of Melbourne. At that
time, she was working as a nurse in the Melbourne hospital.
In his vacillating, self-analytical way he fell in love with her.
He wrote to her all during the second period of his stay in

Boyowa (1917–18) intense, self-revelatory letters in which he tried to tell her all about his inner life. At the same time, he was still writing to another woman in London with whom he had emotional ties. At times he announced to his diary that he considered Elsie Masson to be his future wife, at other times he was not so sure. He sternly tried to repress his erotic impulses toward other women, a weakness which he considered unworthy. "Kenoria is pretty, has a wonderful figure. Impulse to 'pat her on the belly.' I mastered it." The spectacle of the emotional anthropologist solemnly doing Swedish exercises to keep his mind off sex is scarcely less amusing than his own note that he sat in his tent singing a bawdy song to a Wagnerian melody to keep the witches away. He regularly announced in his diary that he had once and for all put his two besetting temptations, novel reading and lecherous thoughts, away from him and, just as regularly, he recorded that he had again succumbed. He referred to his Dostoevskian moods and continued to dose himself because of real or imaginery illnesses.

Despite the frustrations of isolation from the intellectual life that he enjoyed in London and the problems of forcing himself to concentrate on his work, he was learning his trade. He selected a series of "institutions," or what we might call traditional activities or ways of behaving, for study in terms of what he knew about the society as a whole. For instance, his study of gardens and their magic covered a complex of economic, ritual and magical activity which threw light upon the psychology of a people in this particular stage of culture.

Outside the village, where the low, dense jungle grew in a matted tangle, patches were cleared for yam, taro and banana gardens. Early in the year, the sprouting crops were bright green; at harvest time the ripe vines and leaves turned brown. About half the natives' lives were spent in these gardens and much more than half of their interests and ambitions were connected with them. It became clear from his work that just as for "civilized people," for the preliterate, prestige and social approval were the real goals of life. A man of western culture, for instance, buys an automobile in order to transport him to work but the practical use of the car is only part of its human significance. If he has money he spends it on the car for its beauty (as sold to him by advertising) and to give him status among his friends and neighbors. Ownership gives him a sense of power and the feeling that he is keeping up with the Joneses.

The Trobrianders raised twice as many yams as they needed for actual food so they could be piled up at ceremonial feasts to be admired. They then distributed the excess ceremonially to clan relatives. Part of the crop was stowed in yam houses, some was ceremonially exchanged with other villages. Some was merely allowed to rot. This excess of yams created wealth; being in a position to give it away or waste it gave prestige.

Garden magic was a part of island digging-stick and hoe agriculture. A digging-stick was merely a wooden stick, the end pointed and hardened by scorching in the fire. It was used in Africa and the Americas as well as the South Seas by primitive tribesmen. Garden magicians were generally village headmen. These were specialists who were paid for their work. The people as a whole took some part in the ceremonials. There were rites before cutting the scrub, before burning off the underbrush, before planting and weeding, and simply to insure a good crop in general. The magic, they said, had emerged from the ground with their ancestors. Food presents were made to these ancestors and the magicians had to deny themselves certain tabu foods. Spells were sung or chanted and some were not without poetic imagery. Before cutting scrub, the magician chanted:

*The belly of my garden leavens.*
*The belly of my garden rises.*
*The belly of my garden reclines.*
*The belly of my garden grows to the size of a bush hen's nest.*
*The belly of my garden rises like an ant hill.*
*The belly of my garden rises like an ironwood palm.*
*The belly of my garden lies down.*
*The belly of my garden swells.*
*The belly of my garden swells with child.*
*I sweep away.*

The gardeners knew all about the qualities of soil and the need for weeding and cultivation but magic took care of abnormal situations. In this Malinowski disagreed completely with his predecessor, Frazer, who regarded magic as simply an inefficient attempt to be scientific. To Malinowski, who observed the practice of magic in all departments of native life, science was the practical know-how which any intelligent native used in weeding, planting, managing a canoe, or building a house. But, like all men, Europeans or Trobriand Islanders, they knew that uncontrollable things happen. Rain might not come and the gardens would dry up. A tempest might upset their canoes and drown the fishermen. Life was unpredictable and uncertain but they hoped by their traditional spells to control this margin of unpredictability. The missionaries tried to tell them that divine service would make their gardens grow. Malinowski said the Melanesian suspected them, not of lying, but of a certain feeble-mindedness. The parallel, however, was obvious. The westerner prayed that he might not suffer from bad luck or unexpected calamities, the Melanesian thought he had a more reliable system. But magic and religion had the same aims and were products of the same psychological processes.

The repetitive patter of magic spells accompanied almost every activity, from love making to building a canoe. Next to their gardens, canoes were the natives' pride and joy. Small dugout canoes were used for lagoon fishing but they also made large outrigger craft propelled both by sail and leaf-shaped paddles. The lateen sail, hung crosswise from the mast, was constructed by sewing pandanus leaves together and allowed the natives to voyage from island to island. This was a highly adventurous enterprise for they could not beat into the wind and a sudden shift of the wind easily capsized them. Nevertheless, a larger boat of this type, a double canoe with a platform across the gunwales was probably used by their ancestors who left southern Asia to populate New Guinea and the adjacent islands, about 1000 B.C.

The seagoing canoes were used for the curious semiannual ceremonial exchange voyage called the *kula*. This was undertaken when the crops did not need attention and the winds were fairly steady. The trading objects were red shell necklaces and white shell bracelets. They would be carried to a certain island, exchanged and, in turn, carried to a different island and exchanged by the new owner. Thus the objects travelled in a geographical circle. The necklaces, made in the south, travelled counterclockwise among adjacent islands, the bracelets made in the north, travelled clockwise. In theory, they could eventually come back to their original owners. The kula trading partners were friends, patrons, allies. Kula objects might take from two to ten years to make the circle of the islands. The whole formalized, ritual dance involved once more the prestige ownership of the objects which were seldom worn and considered to be historic heirlooms. (Perhaps the only parallel in western culture is the giving of Christmas presents.)

The enterprise started with magic to aid the construction of the canoe which was compared, in the spell, to a flying witch. (Certain women were supposed to be flying witches especially dangerous to sailors for they endeavored to shipwreck them and feast on their bodies.) When the fleet was ready, the mariners dressed in their best with red hibiscus flowers in their thick hair. They also made use of "beauty magic" to make themselves attractive to their kula partners. Before starting they picnicked on the beach, then the flotilla set sail all together. Malinowski described setting out this way:

> Sitting in the slender body while the canoe darts on with the float raised, the platform (across the outrigger) steeply slanting and the water constantly breaking over . . . the sail is hoisted, its stiff heavy folds of gold unroll with a characteristic swishing and crackling noise and the canoe begins to make way when the water rushes away with a hiss and the yellow sail glows against the intense blue of the sea—then indeed the romance of sailing seems to open through a new vista.

The green and white waters were sprinkled with patches of brown seaweed. There were dangerous shoals whose origin was described in myth. Far away could be seen the cloud-wreathed mountains of other islands. As they sailed into new waters the mariners heard the cries of strange birds, the laughing jackass and the melancholy note of the South Sea crow, which never visited Boyowa. The sea became transparent, a pure blue in which they could see brilliant corals and multi-colored fish that were not native to their lagoon.

They passed volcanic islands with boiling springs, composed of dark obsidian rock, yellow ochre and hills of ash. On such an island the mythical hero, Kasabwayreta, was marooned by his companions but escaped by climbing a tree to the sky.

In the old days, the Trobriand voyagers ran the risk of being attacked by cannibal neighbors or an unforeseen current might sweep them out to sea forever. Always imperiled by potential disaster, their voices were raised in monotonous spells to keep the winds favorable. In the midst of a squall, when the canoe tipped threateningly, they were sure they could see flying witches hovering about the rigging, waiting to feast on their drowned corpses.

When the kula voyagers reached their destination, they beached their vessels and were feasted by their hosts. Each partner vied with the other in exchanging the shell ornaments to the sound of conch trumpets. The trading was also done on a credit basis, with promises to pay in objects which they did not yet own. A little subsidiary practical trading went on in pots, or whatever articles the hosts specialized in making, and then the fleet sailed home. The whole expedition combined romance, adventure and increased prestige, the goal for which the Trobrianders lived.

Gardens and kula voyages are two "institutions" studied by Malinowski. Another of these investigations in depth is embodied in a well-publicized book, *The Sexual Life of Savages*, which was not published until 1929. In it the anthropologist assembled data concerning every intimate detail of Trobriand erotic life. In this area he freed himself completely from the tabus in western writing for, in the twenties, sex was still a subject surrounded with considerable prudish hysteria. Malinowski's book was a real breakthrough. The most interesting of his findings, as far as western culture was concerned, was the discovery that premarital affairs were the rule rather than the exception. No censorship was exercised over the sex exploits of young people but the boys and girls were expected to exercise a certain discretion. After a few years of romantic experiment, when an affair had gone on for some time, the couple generally settled down in formal marriage. After marriage, affairs were supposed to cease. The young men, living in the men's house (a sort of club for the unmarried) sometimes took their girls there, or else they made use of corners in yam houses. Sometimes groups of girls went on an expedition to a nearby village and paired off with the boys there. To a westerner the Trobrianders' notion of discretion was odd for, while nobody minded young people sleeping together, eating together in public before marriage was considered a shocking breach of morality.

Malinowski was convinced that the Trobrianders did not understand the father's role in reproduction. They insisted, again and again, that females, whether pigs or human, could produce young without connection with males. Women were impregnated by spirits at night, with pigs it just happened. This rejection of the facts of life, while blaming conception on spirits, has been noted in other preliterate cultures. In northern Australia, a similar view prevailed but William Lloyd Warner had the feeling that there was a kind of wilful rejection of physiological facts because they did not fit into religious dogma.

Marriage involved the consent of the girl's family. Sometimes young people defied adult opinion and married anyway. The ceremony itself consisted in the girl's going to her bridegroom's family dwelling, eating her meals there, sleeping there with him and helping him with his work. So much for ceremony but once more yams came into the picture. The girl's relatives first brought three sets of presents—yams first cooked, then uncooked, then cooked. Then the boy's parents reciprocated with more yams, cooked. Then followed such gifts as stone axe blades and shell necklaces plus more uncooked yams. From then on the families gave presents of yams at harvest time to the young people, when they had built their house, and to each other. More presents continued throughout the marriage; there was no end to the conspicuous yam-giving. It was thought that this continual exchange exerted a binding force on the marriage.

One more important institution investigated by Malinowski was religion. At death, the spirit or *baloma* left the earth to go and live in a shadowy afterworld. Those left behind wailed for him and celebrated an endless series of feasts, also distributing uncooked foods. There was some contradiction as to what happened to the spirit. In one version it led a short and precarious existence near the village, frequenting the man's garden or hanging about the beach. In this version it was called a *kosi*. Sometimes it knocked on the doors of friends or relatives, threw small stones, called out peoples' names or was heard laughing at night. This type of spirit was more of a nuisance than any real danger and, although capable of frightening the living, did not do them any harm.

The real baloma had to meet Topileta, the headman of the village of the dead, on the island of Tuma (about ten miles away). That Tuma was inhabited by live natives did not interfere with belief in it as the location of the afterworld. Beside the dead man were laid all of his most valuable possessions so that he could take their "spirit part" with him. The baloma itself, after leaving the body, sat down and wailed, an activity in which he was joined by his dead kinsmen. It then washed its eyes at a certain well which rendered it invisible and went and knocked on a stone which made the earth tremble. Then the baloma found itself in Tuma. The spirit was met by Topileta who had to be paid for showing the way to the village. It was here that the spiritual parts of the dead man's axe blades and decoration came in handy. Topileta inquired the cause of death and pointed the appropriate road (there were three) which led to the village. A spirit who could not afford payment would be in a bad way and end up turned into a mythical fish with the head and tail of a shark and the body of a sting ray. Topileta himself looked like a man except that he had huge ears which flapped continually. His wife played hostess to female spirits. He had certain magical powers, being able to cause earthquakes and to rejuvenate himself and his family when they grew old.

In Tuma the spirit entered a paradise of food, sex and luxury. The spirit women overwhelmed him with offers of themselves. He, quite willing, participated in orgies of sex. Life was a perfect bacchanal of dancing and chanting in the village square or on the beach. There was a profusion of green coconut drinks, of aromatic leaves and magically potent decorations, of wealth and insignia of honor. By the neatest trick of the week every one became a chief but no chief felt his rank diminished by these magical promotions. Interestingly enough, in this somewhat Moslem-sounding heaven, there was a mechanism for rejuvenation when the spirits became old.

Long ago, when men first came out of the ground, they had been able to cast off their skins like crabs, snakes and lizards but they lost this power through the stupidity of a primal mother. In Tuma, they regained this useful talent and, when old, sloughed off their wrinkles and emerged with smooth skin, sound teeth and rejuvenated appetites for pleasure. This was, of course, the male description of Tuma, which Malinowski never seems to have correlated with evidence from the women.

At any rate, the balomas did not always stay put but were inclined to visit their native villages. Occasionally, they were seen briefly by relatives but their really important migration took place at the *milamila* feast which occurred after the harvest and before it was time to plant again. At this time the yams were dug, cleaned of hairy fibers, piled up to be admired and finally put in the yam houses, some of which sported beautifully decorated gables. In the milamila itself, dancing and drumming took place. In fact, this was the only time of the year at which the natives indulged in such festivities. The men put on white headdresses of cockatoo feathers which looked like a cross between a halo and an American Indian's war bonnet. The feathers were stuck into their bushy hair and overtopped by a plume of red-tipped cassowary feathers. They danced in a circle, raising their legs high, to monotonous chants. Sometimes they used small shields decorated with the same scrolls, in red, white and black, as appeared on the houses and on the sterns of canoes. Sometimes they held streamers of pandanus leaves in their hands. Important dances ended when the sun went down but drumming continued far into the night. At this time many ceremonial visits were exchanged with neighboring villages, presents were given, dances were bought and sold and love affairs took place. During such visits "ceremonial" weapons were carried, reminiscent of the time before colonial intervention when cannibal raids actually took place. These weapons were wooden swords, walking sticks and short spears. They were all beautifully carved in scrolls and complex curvilinear designs so characteristic of the South Seas. Men also painted their faces, a white nose sticking out of a completely black face, one black eye, or a series of complicated curving lines constituting real dandyism.

The balomas knew that the feast began at the first half of the milamila moon (August or September) and sailed over from Tuma to either hang about the houses of relatives or to camp on the beach. Platforms were built by the natives for the spirits to sit on and special displays of food and valuables were set up to please them. Strings of red shells were hung from the roofs, polished axe blades, arm shells and pig teeth necklaces were placed on the platforms. Scaffoldings were also erected on which were hung bunches of bananas, taro roots, exceptionally big yams and coconuts. A parallel exists in our Christmas decorations. Indeed, for the Trobrianders, the milamila was a kind of Christmas and New Year's celebration rolled into one.

Food was offered to the baloma who partook of the spiritual substance, leaving the material part to be eaten by its owners. If the spirits were not adequately entertained they got angry, caused thunder and rain or went to the other extreme and caused a drought which would ruin next year's crops. They also transmitted messages to the living and punished any failure to keep up traditional customs.

The festival ended after two weeks, the second day after the full moon, at which time the baloma had to return home. Their departure was made certain by a ceremonial expulsion. When the morning star appeared, dancing, which had gone on all night, ceased. The drums intoned a special beat, the *ioba*, which the baloma had to obey. Meanwhile the spirits were told

> *Oh spirits, go away,*
> *We shall remain . . .*

This was done in a procession which wound through the whole village, leaving no part of it "unswept." When Malinowski actually witnessed the ceremonial expulsion, he was surprised to find that the drums were beaten by small boys, most people were too sleepy to participate and those who did made jokes and begged the anthropologist for tobacco. Although the ceremony was important and never omitted, there was no sense of awe or solemnity about it. (Malinowski failed to draw the parallel that the western Christmas has also undergone a change from the religious atmosphere of its origin.)

The baloma played still another role in the lives of the islanders. They believed that in certain cases when a baloma had grown old he went to the beach, bathed in the water, threw off his skin and, instead of returning to his youthful but mature shape, became a tiny infant again. A baloma woman seeing this little object, really an embryo, picked it up and put it in a folded coconut leaf. She carried it to the islands and inserted it into the body of some woman who immediately became pregnant. This was the Trobiand explanation of how children came to be conceived.

It can be seen from these descriptions of Trobriand institutions that Malinowski's records of native life were much like a novelist's insights. His method differed in that he checked and rechecked with various informants after a particular observation. For instance, when he was walking home Indian file with three natives from a dead man's house, one of his companions stopped and looked about, as if struck by some strange occurrence. The anthropologist discovered that he was convinced he had detected a kosi in a yam garden they were passing. From this Malinowski pursued his investigation into the natural history of the kosi and tied it up with all other facts he had collected concerning the afterworld.

The approach was described as a well-documented anecdote set in a context of observation which tied it up with all the institutions upon which it shed light. He worked strictly with facts, nearly all of them collected from one specific island culture. This was his weakness and his strength. In his time it was new. He described his material as drawn from three sources: concrete cases, tables and charts to show patterns of relationship, and rituals. Then there were details of emotional reactions gathered from conversations such as likes, dislikes, vanities, ambitions, attitudes toward individuals, in short informative gossip. Finally he collected documentary material such as myths, songs, stories, traditional beliefs.

By the time his stay was over, he was fluent in the native language, had made many friends and had collected a vast amount of data which was to be worked up into several books. He was convinced that he would revolutionize anthropology and yet, strangely enough, his ambivalence was just as strong as ever for, even to the end of his diary, he continued to refer to the Trobrianders with the American word "nigger."

Near the end of his stay in Boyowa, Malinowski's mother died. The news was a great shock to him. Immediately on his return to Melbourne he married Elsie Masson and was apparently again threatened with tuberculosis. In the light of his temperament, there was probably a large psychic element in his illnesses. Indeed, his constant preoccupation with women in his diary indicated that dependence on his mother emotionally had much to do with shaping his life. After his marriage, he went to the Canary Islands to recuperate and, in 1924, he bought a house in northern Italy from which he commuted to London where he was Reader in Social Anthropology at the University of London. He, his wife, and his three daughters moved to London in 1929. During these years, the Trobriand material was published in a series of books which made his name famous. In 1926, he delivered a series of lectures at Cornell University. In 1934, he made a flying trip to Africa and in 1935, his life was darkened by the tragedy of the death of his wife. Elsie Malinowski had been an understanding partner. The end of her life was tragic for she contracted an incurable spinal disease and was bedridden for some ten years. In 1937, Malinowski was again in poor health. He took a sabbatical which he spent in Arizona, taking an interest in the Pueblo Indians whose language he admitted even he found difficult.

During his years as a teacher, Malinowski became almost a legend. He might lie in bed dictating with the top of his pajamas tied about his head, but he would also lead his students about, walking, eating, dodging market barrows on side streets. They even learned to discuss their theses on top of buses as they followed him about London. Although he was a successful popular lecturer and drew large audiences, in the university he abandoned lecturing, ignored the prescribed curriculum and conducted brilliant Socratic seminars on subjects that interested him. These were attended by colonial officials on leave, other university teachers, amateurs and undergraduates. His wit was proverbial, but it often made enemies for it had a satirical bite. He was also deliberately theatrical and fond of shocking people. He once wrote a missionary in language which the recipient of the letter called "so terrible that I can not let my secretary read it."

Malinowski spent his summers in his villa in Overborn, in South Tyrol, overlooking the Dolomites of Northern Italy, among scenery he considered the finest in Europe. Here several students were accustomed to follow him. They lived in a pension near by, set up their writing materials under the trees and worked all day in the open. In the afternoon they went up to the villa where they had tea with him and his new wife and then went walking and discussed progress in their work. After dinner they gathered in the villa to read aloud sometimes Malinowski's own manuscripts, sometimes the work of other anthropologists. Indeed, he always had so many people about him that when he came to London, his wife insisted on buying a country house so that it would be possible at times to enjoy some privacy.

Between Malinowski and Alfred Radcliffe-Brown, the other leader of British anthropology at this time, there was a state of respectful hostility. Each one accepted the other's students without question, they indulged in controversies in scientific journals and, although they both worked in a similar way, were always temperamentally at odds. Malinoswki, however, did not mind being thought an eccentric. His agnosticism, publicly expressed on the BBC, embarrassed his daughters who went to a conventional Church of England school. In addition after one of these broadcasts, the Salvation Army left tracts on his doorstep. Statements like "the eating of decrepit parents is a good method of old-age insurance, while expressing fully an appreciation of one's progenitors" delighted a popular audience and infuriated pedantic scholars. When he wrote "the magnificent title of Functionalist School of Anthropology has been bestowed by myself, in a way on myself and, to a large extent, out of my own sense of irresponsibility," this made still others gnash their teeth at his egotism.

A Chinese student said, "Malinowski is like an Oriental teacher—he is a father to his pupils. He has us to his home; he gets us to run messages for him, sometimes we even cook for him and we like to do these things for him." Yet, there were some former pupils who were critical. One, Max Gluckman, said that he spent too much time demolishing other anthropologists, eventually did the same to his own pupils and was unable to learn from them.

The latter part of his life was spent in America because, once again, he was caught in a foreign country by a war. In 1939, he became a visiting professor at Yale, a position which was made permanent. During this period he began to study the Zapotec Indians of Mexico. He made a study of the activities of the market and planned to use this institution as a center from which to extend his investigations into Indian life. Five years before the end of his life, he was married a second time to an artist, Valetta Swann, who now lives in Mexico. All during World War II, he was a thoroughgoing anti-Nazi with the result that his books were burnt in Germany. On May 15, 1942, in New York he presided as president of the newly formed Polish Institute. The next day, he died in New Haven of a heart attack.

In summing up his work, it is generally agreed that he introduced an interest in social psychology into his field. He also, for the first time, directed the attention of the scholar to the details of ordinary daily existence. Before him anthropologists were concerned with the more striking elements of myth and ritual. Thus he was able, by his study in depth of the life of one group, to show that preliterate men exhibited just as complicated a social life as individuals living in the so-called civilized western world. His critics accused him more than once of developing no system, of never pulling together all his Trobriand material into an organized whole. His excuse was pressure of work and ill-health. Actually a more serious weakness was the fact that whenever he generalized concerning native psychology, he was drawing conclusions exclusively from his Trobriand Islanders. He never bothered to compare his findings with those of investigators working with other cultures.

Not enough credit has been given to him for his influence as a pioneer in applied anthropology. We have seen that Schoolcraft, without knowing it, was an applied anthropologist in that he tried to create a better understanding between the United States government and the American Indians. Not until Malinowski immersed himself in the life of a primitive people in a colonial situation did it occur to ethnologists that their work might serve a practical purpose. Malinowski felt that the scholar could advise the administrator by studying the problems involved in ruling an undeveloped people. He could at least try to prevent a thoughtless outlawing of traditional customs which often destroyed the vitality of the native group. He thought, too, that his science might eventually be able to influence the makers of policy in human relations.

When we try to visualize Malinowski as a man, a most interesting and complex personality emerges. Very sensitive and emotional as he was, it is clear that his unconventionality and occasional arrogance was for him both a defense and a technique for coming to terms with the world. When he felt like it, he could charm and draw out any individual he pleased. One of his daughters described him sitting in a café in Italy while the proprietor and his numerous family poured out their life stories. At the same time, when he became bored with someone, he would simply get up and walk away. When he was giving a course in the New School for Social Research in New York, he found himself confronted with about a hundred students. Since he had no respect for mass methods of education, by skillfully insulting those whom he decided had joined the group for the wrong reasons, he reduced his class to about twenty-five serious scholars. Although he had created a certain role for himself, he was highly self-conscious. Another story, told by his family, describes him as getting into a bitter argument with his daughters about where to go for dinner when he was meeting them for the first time in a year and a half. The girls wanted to dine in luxurious surroundings, he voted for a quiet place where he would have their undivided attention. In the middle of the fight, he suddenly changed his tone and quietly analyzed the motives of both himself and his embattled children. He was notable for being able to do the same thing in the middle of an argument in an academic meeting. Since he was able to step in and out of his public role he was also able to laugh at himself without being afraid to make himself ridiculous. It was this trait which university people, who prize dignity highly, found hard to take. For instance, when a friend found him lying on the floor of the Covent Garden Opera House, during a performance of *Das Rheingold*, he explained calmly that he wanted to hear Wagner and not look at fat Rhine maidens. One of his most important pupils, Raymond Firth, describes a card which Malinowski sent him from Chicago. On it was written, "From the Classical Functionalist School, see lower picture on reverse . . ." (The picture showed two Orangutans drinking from bottles of milk, one bore the initials of Radcliffe-Brown's name, the other Malinowski's initials.) The rest of the card read "to the London Functionalist School, see top picture on reverse." The top picture was a venerable Orang-man sitting in a chair gazing into space and tagged with Firth's initials.

One more quotation from Malinowski's own writing, an article in the journal *Africa* published in 1928, reveals a side of his nature which had much to do with his choice of study and with the motives which cause many anthropologists to immerse themselves in the cultures of exotic groups still untouched by technology. In a spirit of rebellion he wrote:

> Science is the worst nuisance and the greatest calamity of our days. It has made us into robots, into standardized interchangeable parts of an enormous mechanism. It pushes us with a relentless persistence and a terrible acceleration towards new forms of existence . . . an ever-increasing speed in communication; accessibility of superficial knowledge and meretricious art; endless opportunities in cheap and mean forms of amusement, leisure to do a thousand irrelevant things—these, from the side of human consumption and enjoyment, are the benefits of civilization. . . . Anthropology, to me at least, was a romantic escape from our overstandardized culture.

**4**

# CLAUDE
# LÉVI-STRAUSS

Claude Lévi-Strauss is today the leading French anthropologist. He is also a leading French intellectual, a man who has developed a school of anthropology called "structuralism" which has become something of a fad in sophisticated Parisian circles. Since it is the fashion to be a structuralist, various people apply the word to themselves even though they have only a remote acquaintance with his work. Now that his books have been translated into English he is much discussed by Americans and he has become a rather controversial figure.

He was born in 1908. His grandfather was rabbi of Versailles and it was with this grandparent that he lived during the period of World War I. By the age of twelve he was an unbeliever but he tells us that religion was taken lightly in his home and the prayers before meals impressed him less than a long strip of paper in the dining room with the legend, "Chew your food properly: your digestion depends on it." Two of his uncles were painters of academic portraits and landscapes, which perhaps accounts for his familiarity with and interest in painting. Looking back, he feels that the impact of a different culture first struck him when his father gave him a

Japanese print as a reward for doing well in school when he was six. When he entered the Sorbonne, he was still uncertain what he wanted to be. He began the study of philosophy, for which he was well suited, but soon began to feel that this subject, as it was taught in the Sorbonne, was a pointless game. He read Freud, whose work convinced him that the workings of the mind had more reality than the academic studies that had already bored him. He also read Karl Marx, but neither of these thinkers seem to have influenced his later work. In 1928, during Lévi-Strauss's first year at the Sorbonne, Frazer paid his last visit to Paris and gave a memorable lecture but Lévi-Strauss was still indifferent to anthropology. It took the study of geology and the fact that his parents bought a house in the Cévennes mountains to draw him toward natural science. In the country he would disappear on fifteen-hour walks, forgetting time while he studied a dandelion or searched for the stratification line between two deposits of limestone.

Lévi-Strauss has been quoted as saying that scholars probably undertake the study of other cultures because they are dissatisfied with their own. He added that he was not impressed by the one he grew up in. We therefore assume that in his young manhood he was going through a certain amount of questioning of values and rebellion against his environment. As a result of a great deal of serious thinking, he turned toward anthropology. In France, the basis of this study had been laid by Emile Durkheim, who also is called the father of sociology, Marcel Mauss and A. Van Gennep. Lévi-Strauss does not seem to have been immediately drawn to their work. Instead, he began reading a book by an American, Robert H. Lowie's *Primitive Society*. Here he learned concrete facts about human beings, facts which had real meaning for him. Lowie was a pupil of the great American anthropologist Franz Boas, as was Alfred Kroeber. Lévi-Strauss became familiar with the works of these scholars.

He had meanwhile changed from philosophy to law but decided the latter study was equally tiresome. After five years at the Sorbonne, he became a teacher in provincial schools. He discovered, to his dismay, that, as the curriculum did not change, he would have to give essentially the same lectures over and over again. The prospect horrified him.

It so happened that he had been an outstanding pupil of George Dumas who taught psychology at the Sorbonne. Dumas was a grand old man with a shock of white hair who gave brilliant impromptu lectures and had a background of teaching in Brazil.

Lévi-Strauss's escape from secondary school teaching and into his profession came about in dramatic form. At nine o'clock of a Sunday morning in the autumn of 1934, a friend of his, who was director of the École Normal Supérieure, called him up and, speaking for Dumas, asked him if he still wanted to be an anthropologist. Since the answer was yes, he was told to apply for the post of professor of sociology at São Paulo University. "The outskirts are full of Indians and you can spend your weekends studying them" his friend went on, "but you must give Georges Dumas a definite answer before twelve this morning."

He accepted enthusiastically. French anthropology was mostly theoretical at this time and the chance to do field work in South America was a godsend. "I imagined Brazil as a tangled mass of palm leaves, with glimpses of strange architecture in the middle distance, and an all-permeating smell of burning perfume."

São Paulo was a new university which Dumas was helping to staff, but the old psychology professor's information about the inhabitants was inaccurate. There were no Indians in the suburbs. In fact, Lévi-Strauss was to encounter some rather shocking attitudes towards them. The Brazilian ambassador told him, "Alas, my dear Sir, the Indians have all been dead and gone for many a year. It's a sad page—yes, and a shameful one—in the history of my country. But the Portuguese colonists in the sixteenth century were a brutal money-grabbing lot. Who are we to reproach them if they behaved as every one else behaved at that time? They used to grab hold of the Indians, tie them to the cannon's mouth and blow them to pieces. That's how they went, every man Jack of them."

Actually, this shifting the blame to the sixteenth century covered up a sense of guilt that must have been profound. The ambassador's own forefathers and even some of his contemporaries had other means of exterminating Indians. They used to call at the hospital for clothes which had belonged to patients who died of smallpox. These they would mingle with the usual type of presents given to primitives, mirrors and beads, and throw them along the pathways used by the natives. By means of this biological warfare a brilliant result was achieved. In 1918, two-thirds of the state of São Paulo (as big as France) was marked as unexplored territory inhabited only by Indians. By the time of Lévi-Strauss's arrival, in 1935, not a single Indian was left. In reduced numbers, however, Indians continued to live in the vast interior of the country, an area practically unsettled and very hard to penetrate.

The Frenchman's first impression of the Brazilian coast was an enormous range of mountains, crags of polished stone which went on repeating themselves in an endless series of crests. It was his introduction to the scale of the New World—a sense of man dwarfed by the landscape which Europeans feel very keenly. And, indeed, even North Americans visiting South America feel it too, for civilization occurs in little pockets and corners, dwarfed by the great central mountain chain, the jungles and deserts.

The students at the University of São Paulo were the children of a new and insecure middle class. Some of them were

already professionals who wanted a degree in order to compete with rivals and hoped to shed their countrified manners.
They wanted to hear about the latest ideas rather than to learn
about the past. Traditionally Paris had been the city toward
which they looked for culture (the children of the wealthy
had been sent there for their education). Thus the new French
teachers arrived with enormous prestige. Around each, little
admiring groups collected and these competed in giving lunch-
eons or tea parties for their Parisian heroes.

Brazilian cities impressed Lévi-Strauss by the fact that, in
this warm climate, life spilled out upon the street. The houses
themselves took him back into the nineteenth century. Built
on a terrain a couple of thousand feet in altitude, São Paulo
is not altogether tropical although it has a tropical rainy season.
Villas of painted wood rotted in gardens of mango and euca-
lyptus trees. A long avenue ran between Syrian bazaars and
workshops where tooled leather saddles and harnesses, embellished with chased silver, were made for the planters who rode
about in the "bush." The very wealthy lived in a suburb to
the south where they had built California-style houses with
wrought-iron balustrades. These houses were set in thick plots
of woodland. There was a park in the wealthy section designed
along English lines, with lawns embellished with statues and
summer houses. At the edge of it rose the city's most preten-
tious buildings, the municipal theater, the Hotel Esplana, the
Automobile Club and the offices of the Canadian Electric
Company.

Between São Paulo and its seaport, Santos, the country was
a network of wet flatlands, swamps, rivers, canals and lagoons.
In the plantations could be seen the sharp green of bananas
waving their long fronds which often looked like torn sails.
In the forest itself, the leaves were a dark jade or emerald
against which the grey or whitish trunks stood out like dried

bones against the green background. Lévi-Strauss, who was well acquainted with modern art, was reminded of canvases by the painter, Henri Rousseau, known as *le Douanier*.

To the north and east was the undeveloped interior. A certain amount of mining had destroyed patches of forest and then the mining had died out, leaving here and there a richly decorated eighteenth-century church to fall into decay. Bits of railroad ran through areas where there were no centers of population. Since South America by the thirties had already begun to leap into the age of the airplane, road building had tended to be stifled. There were, however, tracks through the bush which led to small hamlets which served the plantation owners. Over these the truck or jeep was replacing the mule train and oxcart but the mechanical vehicles had to travel for hundreds of miles over the rough terrain in second or first gear. Along the waterways, a few other towns were connected with civilization by old-fashioned paddle-wheel steamers which dated in style to American riverboats of the mid-nineteenth century. Sometimes, when the trails branched, there was no knowing which was the right road and the unfortunate traveller might go on for hours only to end in a swamp. In the rainy season, the track turned into a canal of greasy mud; then, when the first truck got through, it would leave ruts that hardened in the clayey soil as if carved out of cement. The vehicles which followed had to navigate as best they could over these iron-edged waves. Consequently, trucks were generally manned by two men, one a mechanic, who continually made emergency repairs.

Lévi-Strauss's first trip was straight inland to visit a tribe, the Caduveo, who lived on highlands above the banks of the Tibagy River. There were about 540 of these Indians in five or six villages. The anthropologist travelled with the district commissioner of the Indian's Protection Service, an institution which had been set up historically too late and did too little. It had tried in this particular case to corral the natives into villages and to "integrate them into modern life." The integrating consisted of setting up two or three shops and a school and sending them axes, knives, nails, clothing and blankets. The Indians were then left to their own devices. After twenty years, the Protection Service gave up practically all of its services. The Brazilian government had grown tired of it.

Lévi-Strauss rode with his companions for hours through the jungle, up and down mountains, through streams, at night simply giving his horse its head. When he arrived at the Caduveo villages, he learned what had happened as a result of this long-range brush with civilization. All that remained to the people were their Brazilian clothes, the use of the axe, knife, thread and needle. Houses had been built for them; they preferred to live in the open. They were supposed to live in villages but they were still nomads. They had broken up their beds for firewood and gone back to sleeping on the ground. The herd of cows sent by the government had been allowed to disappear into the jungle; the Indians had never learned to drink milk or eat beef. They were still filing their teeth and clinging to debased forms of their old culture. Since they were no longer "a danger to society," society had forgotten about them. They knew about matches, which they could not afford, and still made fire by rubbing two sticks together. They had been given some rifles and pistols, but these hung in the long-abandoned houses while the Indians still used the bow and arrow. The children went naked.

The ranchers with whom the travellers stopped on their way to the Caduveo villages, regarded the Indians as idlers, degenerates, thieves and drunkards. They were amazed when the anthropologist returned later with wooden sculptured figures, huge ceramic jars, engraved and painted deer hides decorated with arabesques. It was in the Indians' artistic tradition, particularly the face painting, that Lévi-Strauss found the key to the life of these Indians and to their image of themselves in the past.

The plain on which they lived was watery, crossed by a marshy river that seemed to have neither source nor mouth. On this treeless area they had built their own type of house, four-forked uprights with a thatched roof, each sheltering several families. Apparently they had a tradition of "long houses" similar to those used by the Iroquois in New York State.

The pottery was made by the women by the coil method (that is, coils of clay built up the pot which was then scraped thin). Then impressions were made on it with string to outline the design, painted with red iron oxide. It was finally baked over a fire and, while hot, given a couple of coats of resin varnish. The wooden statuettes seemed to vary in use from dolls to idols. One or two could be connected with well-known myths, the Mother of Twins and the Little Old Man. The local witch doctor, who wore a headdress of straw and used a gourd rattle, occupied himself with capturing spirits who caused illness. Suspicious of the foreigners, he refused to sell them any religious objects.

Rituals, such as the puberty festival of young girls, were celebrated by drinking parties at which the natives sang and made speeches. Often these affairs degenerated into bouts of weeping, hysterical laughter and incoherence. "In the 1930s these ragged peasants were a pitiable sight in their forlorn and marshy habitat; but their wretchedness made it all the more striking that they have clung tenaciously to some vestige of their ancestral customs."

By combining his own observations with reports from earlier travellers, Lévi-Strauss was able to reconstruct the picture of a curiously artificial society. In the past, these people had been warriors and head-hunters. They had enslaved a weaker people, the Guana, and considered themselves to be aristocrats divided into castes: commoners, great hereditary nobles, and individuals who had been raised to the nobility. These aristocrats were admitted into a warrior brotherhood which entitled them to special names and a special cult language. They wore a handsome dress, a tunic of leather which broadened at their shoulders and hung stiffly down at the sides and was painted in designs of red and black. The Guana tilled the soil and paid their lords tribute in return for "protection" like the feudal peasants of Europe.

The nobles quite literally bore "the mark of their rank" in the form of pictorial designs—painted or tattoed—on their bodies. They were the equivalent of a coat of arms. The nobles plucked out their facial hair—eyebrows and lashes included—and recoiled in disgust from the bushy-browed European: "the ostrich's brother" was their name for him. Men and women alike were accompanied in public by a suite of slaves and hangers-on; these vied with one another to spare the then lords all effort.

The arrogance of these Indian aristocrats even impressed the Portuguese for certain noble ladies refused to meet the wife of the viceroy; only the queen of Portugal, they said, was worthy to associate with them.

In this tribe the men were sculptors, the women painters. In 1935, the best women artists were "hideous old monsters, heavily made up and weighted down with trinkets who excused themselves for having had to give up their former accomplishments, now that they were deprived of their slaves." Nevertheless, Lévi-Strauss was able to collect 400 designs, some of which could be compared with those collected in the past (forty years before), so tenacious was this key element in their culture. The face and sometimes the body was covered with a network of asymmetrical scrolls, spirals, frets and curlicues. Since the natives demanded money for photographs, Lévi-Strauss drew outlines of faces on sheets of paper and gave them to the old ladies to decorate. They did it with ease. They could start at any corner and cover the area with a perfectly balanced design which centered on elaborate flourishes around the mouth. Even though this people was dying out, the anthropologist was to receive, fifteen years later, a collection of these designs made by a Brazilian among which were many of the same patterns he himself had gathered.

It was fascinating to remember that these decorated nobles carried out festivities in which warriors were served with liquor in goblets made from horns or skulls. Heralds would call out family titles. Women would borrow warriors' armor and play at mimic warfare. The nobles, seated in order of precedence, were served by slaves. Their task "was to help their masters to vomit, in due course, and to watch over them until they finally fell asleep in search of delicious visions which drink would procure for them."

Interestingly enough, the Caduveo myth of creation was remarkably frank about their role in the world. When the trickster-creator god brought people from the earth, the slave Guana came first and were given agriculture. Other tribes were assigned to hunting activities, but finally he noticed the Caduveo, forgotten in the bottom of the hole. There was only one task left, he gave them the role of ruling and enslaving others. They were to reign over the rest of the human race.

Lévi-Strauss was interested in the relation of the Caduveo facing or tattooing to other similar practices in North America, also connected with rank, particularly among the Northwest Indians. In general face painting "conferred upon the individual his dignity as a human being: they help him cross the frontier from Nature to Culture, and from the 'mindless' animal to the civilized man. Furthermore, they differ in style and composition according to social status and thus have a social function."

There was one local result of the anthropologist's work.

When he returned by way of the cattle-raiser's hacienda, his hosts became converted to Caduveo art. He learned later that they began to tolerate Indians on the premises and eventually decorated their living room with ceramics and ornamented hides.

Near the border of Bolivia, on the Paraguay River, navigated by small paddle-wheel steamers and canoes, lay Corumba, a town perched on the top of a limestone cliff. The town had once been of more importance when there had been some traffic between the interior and the Rio de la Plata. Now, with its long streets of flat-roofed houses, painted white or beige, it somehow had the atmosphere of a ghost town in the American West. To reach the Bororo, a tribe far into the interior, Lévi-Strauss took one of the little steamers, whose passengers, because of the hot weather, changed into their beach attire, striped pajamas. After eight days of rice and black beans with guava jelly for dessert and sometimes whole days lost pulling the vessel off of mud flats, the steamer reached Cuiaba, the capital of the state. The only diversions during the trip were watching the blue, red and gold parrots flit by or throwing unbaited hooks into the water to catch the bloodthirsty piranhas. Cuiaba was a faded eighteenth-century town created by gold and diamonds. Small nuggets could be sieved out of the river or even turned up when gardening. Diamond hunters haunted the bush like the Alaskan gold prospectors of the Yukon, but their wares were rigidly inspected and regulated by the government.

Lévi-Strauss was told by the local bishop that he knew all about the Indians. They were not as stupid as one might think. One Bororo woman had actually been converted. It was suggested that the anthropologist give them no presents except axes to remind them of the sacredness of work.

The next phase of the trip was by truck, and a gruelling journey it was. Whole days were spent laying floors of logs ahead of the vehicle to get it through swamps. When navigating sand, the travellers had to stuff leaves and branches under the wheels. The truck drivers knew how to live off the land. When they shot a deer, they cut out the meat into strips and dried it in the wind or sun so that it would keep, precisely as did the Plains Indians of the United States.

Through the flatlands rough, milky-green grass and a few gnarled shrubs only partly concealed the pinkish sand. When inundated in the rainy season, the grass would turn bright green and the trees would be covered with white and mauve flowers. When the expedition met diamond hunters, the group would camp and the frontiersmen would do comic turns or sing. One song dealt with the private who complained about army rations. The corporal "took up his pen" and passed the complaint on to the lieutenant. It went all the way up to the general and finally the emperor who passed it on to Jesus Christ and finally:

> Jesus Christ who is the son of the father eternal
> Took up his pen and consigned them all to regions infernal.

The journey became a nightmare, a continual loading and unloading of the vehicles, laying planks, sleeping on the bare ground, ridding their clothes of termites which would riddle them with holes. The road became doubtful and the anthropologist was almost ready to turn back. When, at last, the party came to a few huts, they blew their horns in triumph. Not a soul came to meet them. Finally, after much scouting in the outskirts, one family was found. The population had moved out because of an epidemic of yellow fever. The head of the family agreed to provide canoes for a trip up the river which took eight days and involved the killing of a twenty-one-foot boa constrictor.

Finally the canoes put in to shore at a clay bank at the top of which a few huts could be seen.

> We were welcomed with fits of laughter by a group of naked men, painted red with urucuru from their toe nails to the roots of their hair. They helped us to disembark, grabbed hold of our luggage and conducted us to a large hut in which several families were living. There the chief of the village made over his own corner to us; and for the duration of our visit, he went to live on the opposite bank of the river.

The chief did not know or pretended not to know Portuguese. Although he courteously took care of the needs of the travellers, he never communicated with Lévi-Strauss directly but always through the members of his council. The anthropologist's interpreter was Kejara, the show Indian of the missionaries, who had been taught to read and write and sent to Rome to meet the Pope. Unfortunately, when the monks tried to marry him with Christian rites, he underwent a religious crisis and returned to the faith of his fathers. He was now naked, painted red, his lip and nose pierced by ornamental mother-of-pearl plugs and wore a feathered headdress. His training, however, made him an excellent informant concerning Bororo culture.

Body painting was the required wardrobe of a Bororo male. On top of the basic red, horseshoe patterns were sometimes added in black resin. White down was also stuck to the arms or shoulders. The feathered headdresses flared out in a halo around the head. Dancers sometimes wore thick costumes of leaves, covering them from head to foot, that made them look like walking haystacks.

The key characteristic of the Bororo culture was continual preoccupation with religious ritual carried out by the men who all slept in the men's house at night and gathered there during the day when they were not hunting or fishing. The men's house, which we shall mention again in connection with Margaret Mead's Tschambuli, is an institution found among preliterates all over the world, in the South Seas, in Africa, in the Americas. When a warrior-hunter ideal is developed, the magical influence of women is considered to have a bad effect on men's bravery and men's activities in general. Women are generally not allowed to touch weapons or fishing equipment. To protect their male magic the men, therefore, live together and devote only a part of their time to their wives and families.

Lévi-Strauss, exhausted from this trip, was immediately made aware of Bororo piety. The men all began to sing, heavily accented, low-pitched, gutteral songs in unison, alternating with solo passages, with many repetitions. Lévi-Strauss was reminded of a German student singing society. He was told that before the game his party had brought could be eaten, the spirits had to be placated and the chase consecrated. The anthropologist fell asleep on the wings of song, but he was to hear similar rituals almost every evening. The accompanying instruments were calabashes, full of pebbles and flutes.

The next morning, the anthropologist almost stumbled over some pathetic defeathered birds. These were macaws, tamed and plucked at intervals to provide for the feather headdresses. Those on the ground looked ready to be roasted. Others on roof tops had regrown their red and blue feathers.

Much of the character of Bororo society depended on a circular arrangement of huts divided down the middle into two halves or, as they are called in anthropology, *moieties*. Each man belonged to his mother's group and had to marry into the other half. The halves were also subdivided into three clans, each originally divided into three classes and supposed to live in alternating groups of huts. In the center of the village stood the men's house, the space in front of it being used as the dancing ground.

This sort of elaboration, which is not unusual among preliterate groups, had to do with marking off social classes (just as did the face painting among the Caduveo). Apparently men find ways to dominate their fellows through warlike exploits, amassing riches, or by setting up artificial hereditary ranks, whether they be European grand dukes or naked Indians. What amazed anthropologists, when they first discovered this human trait in "savages," was the fact that people without writing were able to hand down complicated hereditary distinctions. The precise arrangement of the huts was one of these aids to memory devised to preserve such intricate forms of aristocracy.

Aside from the prestige of merely being born into a specific clan or group, each group had its particular myths, traditions, dances or rituals, which amounted to non-material wealth. Some clans were also rich in household objects while others were poor, some were sophisticated, some were the equivalent of rural peasants. And all this social elaboration existed among a few hundred naked Indians in a fast vanishing tribe!

The Bororo were great dandies. The women handed down their necklaces of monkey teeth or pendants made of jaguar teeth mounted on wood from generation to generation. Their husbands removed the hair from the women's temples to make ropes which they wore around their own heads like turbans. The men also made pendants from the great claws of the giant armadillo. Aside from the formal macaw headdress they improvised all sorts of decorations, a toucan's beak fastened to a feathered stalk, cylindrical crowns of eagles' feathers mounted on a stick could be six feet tall. They put flowers in their hair and devised earrings from bark and feathers. In all of this display they were as creative as a Parisian milliner. Despite this love of finery, these decorated dandies were utterly masculine in temperament and built like stevedores.

The Bororo had complicated notions concerning death. They believed that their human shape was transitory halfway between a fish and the macaw. When anyone died, it was considered that an injury had been done to the dead man by forces of nature. After the event, a hunt was organized during which it was necessary to kill some sizeable creature such as a jaguar. Then the man's *mori*, the evil which killed him, would be incarnated in the animal killed. Since the spirit would also be filled with hostility toward the hunter who killed it, he would have to paint himself black to escape its notice.

The Bororo spirit world was well populated. Some supernaturals were in control of the stars and the weather, some of sickness and death; in life they had all been sorcerers. Some had holes in their heads from which tobacco smoke poured when they smoked, some had immensely long nails with rain pouring from their eyes, nostrils and hair, some were one-legged with huge bellies and the soft, downy bodies of bats.

The *bari*, or sorcerer, was able to turn into an animal, generally a jaguar, had an animal guardian spirit, and was able to foresee illness and death. A beneficent witch doctor, The Master of Spirits, had similar powers but was able to heal.

The Bororo, with their elaborate dances in which one moiety represented the spirits of the dead and the other strove against them, with their handsome and elaborate rituals, their magnificient singing and love of sophisticated self-decoration, were the most socially healthy tribe which Lévi-Strauss was to visit. Free of missionary and government interference, they were still at peace with nature and their own society, able to live relatively satisfactory lives on their own terms.

In the year which followed, Lévi-Strauss returned to France to write up and publish his material. He also lectured and showed some of his collections in an art gallery. Two leading anthropologists, Henry Mauss and Lucien Lévy-Bruhl, gave him their blessing. Paul Rivet, Director of the Paris Anthro-

pological Museum, also indicated that he approved of his
work. In 1939, Lévi-Strauss obtained funds for another expedition to the interior of Brazil in order to study the tribes in
the Central Plateau. He felt that all of these tribes (including
the Bororo) belonging to the Ge-group were probably the
earliest inhabitants of the southern continent. At some later
date, Brazil had been invaded from the northern coast and
through the Orinoco and Amazon by warlike groups from the
Caribbean. He was much impressed by similarities in culture
between the Brazilian forest people and other tribes of North
and Central America. In his book *A World on the Wane*, he
points out that the early history of the Americas is still in its
infancy because studies of the whole hemisphere are still so
fragmentary.

Back in Cuiaba, the old river town, he learned something
of the recent history of the Nambikwara, his next objective.
A telegraph line to Cuiaba had been finished in 1924 and
almost immediately made useless by the spread of radio communication. The line continued to be feebly kept up, the poles
were falling, the wire was rusting, but a few employees were
left here and there who had neither the courage nor the means
to go elsewhere. The record of contacts between the telegraph
employees and the Nambikwara was discouraging. Some of
the Brazilians visited a native village and were not heard of
again. In 1933, some uninformed missionaries came and
settled in the area. In their attempts to give medical service
they lost a patient. The Indians decided they were poisoners
and massacred six. When Lévi-Strauss contacted one telegraph
station, he was told it had just been threatened with an attack.
Lévi-Strauss, however, was undaunted. He knew well enough
that an anthropologist of experience can generally make peaceful contacts where often untrained missionaries with more zeal
than common sense end up as shrunken heads.

Lévi-Strauss organized an expedition of fifteen men, fifteen mules and thirty oxen. He had three scientific companions. The oxen were given such colorful names as Piano, Mudsquasher, Big Rooster, Palm Tree and Navigator by their drivers.

The trip was, as usual, gruelling. When the scientist's truck broke its drive shaft, the party had to wait for eight days, which incidentally gave the oxen time to catch up. Lévi-Strauss passed the time listening to tall stories, told by his drivers. Added to the heat was the annoyance of stingless bees which continually settled on their faces. The only redeeming incident was the discovery of the insects' store of honey.

They eventually arrived at the Rio Papagaio (Parrot River)

A hundred or more yards wide, with its waters, flowing by at ground level, so clear that we could see deep, deep down to the rocky river bed. On the far side, a handful of straw huts and mud-walled sheds, the Utiarity telegraph station. We unloaded the truck, sent over our luggage and our stores of food by the raft which served as a ferry, and took leave of our drivers. Already on the farther shore we could glimpse the naked bodies of the Nambikwara.

These Indians were nomads but a score or so had just arrived and encamped a few yards away. While they remained in one place (during the rainy season), they planted gardens and raised maize, tobacco, beans, cotton and gourds. They also made much of the manioc, a starchy root which takes the place of potato. At the beginning of the dry season, they split up into small roving bands which subsisted on any small game they could find: grubs, spiders, lizards, grasshoppers, rodents, snakes, along with fruit, seeds, roots and honey. Their shelters consisted of a few branches stuck in the ground and tied at the top to keep off the sun. In hunting they used bows and arrows, tipping the latter with the poisonous curare. These utterly naked people, scarcely over five feet tall, with almost no material possessions and no real houses, seemed, in contrast to the sophisticated and wealthy Bororo, almost in a state of childlike innocence. Their knives were splinters of bamboo or roughly chipped stone. They had a few axes given them by the government but they still used their stone axes as grinders. Pottery was unknown. They had no canoes, when they came to water, they swam across it. All their possessions were slung in plaited bamboo baskets which the women carried on their backs. On the march, they looked like a column of ants carrying their eggs.

Lévi-Strauss encountered one amusing situation as a result of the magic qualities of personal names. The Nambikwara kept theirs secret. All over the world names are felt to be a part of the person himself. As Sir James Frazer had noted, according to the principles of magic, getting hold of a person's name was considered to be a way of affecting him magically. One of the children with whom the anthropologist played had a fight with one of her companions and told him her enemy's name in reprisal. Then the enemy told him the first child's name. Soon the children all became accomplices and from them he also learned the names of adults. Even children can contribute to anthropology although, in this case, the scientist felt slightly embarrassed because of the way he took advantage of them.

When he came to learn something of the Nambikwara language, he felt there were parallels between it and the group of tongues spoken by the Chibcha, who had developed a rather high city culture in Colombia. This and the physical aspect of the small but rather delicately featured Indians made him suspect that they may not always have lived under such poverty-stricken conditions. They might have regressed from a more affluent state of culture because of the environment they had come to inhabit.

The men of this tribe hunted, the women and children

gathered small game and vegetable foods. A little spinning, weaving and grating of manioc completed the household crafts. They also trimmed, polished and strung nuts and river shells as ornaments. Children did little work. The families were cheerful and enjoyed joking and playfully wrestling. Parents played with their children but neither knew any formal games. The growing girls banded together in a group while boys were more inclined to imitate and help their fathers. The whole camp was full of pets: dogs, chickens, monkeys, parakeets, birds, wildcats, coatis.

Lovemaking was relaxed and surrounded by no tabus. Polygamy was occasionally practiced but in most cases there was no surplus of women. On the whole, the little band lived on a subsistence basis and often they subsisted on what seemed almost nothing to a white man. A whole family might dine on a few fleshy fruit from a palm tree, two large poisonous spiders, a lizard or two with their tiny eggs, a bat, some palm nuts and a handful of locusts.

The men had their magic flutes, which could not be seen by women, like the other groups whom Lévi-Strauss encountered. This, too, suggested that their society had once been more complicated.

The Indians were quite willing to discuss the misunderstanding which had resulted in the slaughter of the missionaries. Since they made poisoned arrows themselves and went in for magical poisoning, they had been suspicious of foreigners. Toward Lévi-Strauss they were friendly. He wrote:

> Always they are haunted by the thought of other groups, as fearful and hostile as they are themselves, and when they lie entwined together, couple by couple, each looks to his mate for support and comfort and finds in the other a bulwark, the only one he knows, against the difficulties of every day. . . . In one and all may be glimpsed a great sweetness of nature, a profound

nonchalance, and animal satisfaction as ingenuous as it is charming, and, beneath all this something that can be recognized as
one of the most moving and authentic manifestations of human
tenderness.

There were about two thousand of these Indians left when
Lévi-Strauss visited them. Since then their number has been
steadily reduced by epidemics of influenza against which they
have no defense. Unfortunately, while Lévi-Strauss was among
the Nambikwara, a severe eye disease broke out. It spread to
his bearers and finally to his wife who had been helping him
collect data. Before he left, however, he learned something of
the relationship between bands and of the office of chief.

Since different groups were potentially hostile, when they
came together they exchanged ritual challenges. Finally, when
they had calmed down, they began to barter. They did not
haggle, however, each trader gave what he felt like giving.
This, then, could result in more disagreements and more feelings of hostility.

The authority of a chief was precarious. His title meant "one
who binds together." Although he got the largest share of
presents, he was supposed to have a surplus of food and goods
to give away to the tribesmen when they asked for them. Thus
he seldom had much for himself. If he failed to see to it that
the band was fed and protected from other groups the chances
were that his group would break up. He prepared the curare
for hunting and made the rubber ball they used in sports. He
had to be able to sing and dance so that he could keep up the
spirits of the group when they were bored and unhappy. He
had to know the terrain they inhabited perfectly and to understand the habits of game and know all about the fruit and
vegetable products on which they subsisted. As a consolation
for these heavy responsibilities, he was given one or two of the
prettiest girls as secondary wives but these were partners in
love and did not do the hard work required of the first wife.

Both of the chiefs whom Lévi-Strauss knew well, were highly intelligent capable men. They were his best informants and, in their turn, were always interested in learning from him.

In the light of the romantic theories of early anthropologists and of Sigmund Freud, who believed that a dominant old man, a violently aggressive and polygamous patriarch was the most ancient form of government, Lévi-Strauss was impressed by the fact that these very simple people were not governed by an autocrat but by a man whose power was conditional, whose position was a balance of obligations and privileges and whose life was a series of problems which he took as seriously as any modern prime minister. Lévi-Strauss writes that he was looking for a society reduced to its simplest expression. "The society of the Nambikwara had been reduced to a point at which I found nothing but human beings."

Most of the trip back was by river. Along the way he met a tribal group, the Tupi-Kawahib, a band that had never been studied before. Unfortunately, he encountered this virgin territory when he was exhausted, his bearers worn out from fever and his supplies limited. Since he knew nothing of the language of these people, it would have taken him months to do a proper study. Regretfully he spent a few days learning some words, viewing their maize gardens and their large conical communal houses, made of poles bent together and fastened at the top, and then passed on. These people were a part of the Tupi group of cannibals, who had first been encountered by travellers in the Renaissance. Indeed, the great French essayist Montaigne had written one of his treatises after a conversation with some Tupis who had been brought to Rouen, France.

Later he was to take one last trip through the forest to meet another band of Tupis, with a guide and an interpreter. On this journey he was somewhat hampered by a pet monkey, Lucinda. She was small and grey with a prehensile tail. Mon-

keys are often worn as a headdress in the jungle, for, captured
when young, they are accustomed to cling to the fur of their
mother's back and easily transfer to the hair on a human
being's head. Lévi-Strauss had fed Lucinda on spoonfuls of
condensed milk and she learned to settle for his left boot
instead of his hair. This was all right when riding or travelling in a canoe but when walking through the jungle, with
every inequality of the ground she let out a loud wail. Unfortunately, she could no longer be induced to ride on the
anthropologist's head, so he had to limp along to the accompaniment of Lucinda's dismal cries.

While Lévi-Strauss stayed with this small Tupi group and
gathered what data he could from a dying culture, he was
fortunate enough to witness a performance by the chief like
nothing he had yet experienced. This chief, quite unlike those
he had met in other tribes, was more like a witch doctor in
character in that he seemed somewhat emotionally unbalanced
and prone to possession by spirits. A few nights before Lévi-
Strauss was to leave, the chief stretched out in his hammock
and began to sing! Gradually, as the performance went on, he
began to sing in different voices with an occasional passage
of spoken dialogue. Lévi-Strauss realized that the man was an
inspired poet and he was singing a play in which each actor
was individualized by his voice: high-pitched, squeaky, gutteral, or organlike, with each character having a recurring
musical theme. It was a comedy about the oriole, character-
ized as a trickster, who outwitted the other animals: tortoise,
jaguar, falcon, anteater, tapir, lizard. The audience shouted
with laughter and was so entranced that it was hard to get
them to interpret what was being sung. The performance went
on for two evenings, lasting four hours each time. Sometimes,
when the chief's inspiration waned, several other members of
the tribe would act as a kind of chorus, or take up the dialogue
to get him started. It was clear to Lévi-Strauss that the poet

was a man possessed for the different characters became so individualized that he could recognize them easily. Finally, at the end of the second evening, the chief got out of his hammock still singing, grabbed his knife, and ran after his wife, completely out of control. He was held down by the others, forced back to his hammock in which he fell asleep to arise next morning back to normal.

The journey back to comparative civilization was broken by a long halt because most of the party fell sick. This frustration caused Lévi-Strauss to enumerate some of the hardships of his profession.

> Field work is taxing enough even in normal conditions: the anthropologist must get up at first light and remain alert until the last of his natives has gone to sleep (even then he has to watch over their slumber). He must try to pass unnoticed, and yet always be at hand. He must see everything, remember everything, take note of everything. He must be ready to make the most of a humiliating indiscretion, to go to some snotty-nosed urchin and beg for information, and keep himself ever in readiness to profit by a moment of compliance or free-and-easiness. Or, it may well be, for days together a fit of ill humor among the natives will compel him to shut down on his curiosity and simulate sombre reserve. The investigator eats his heart out in the exercise of his profession: he has abandoned, after all, his environment, his friends and habits, spent a considerable amount of money and time, and compromised his health. And the only apparent result is that his presence is forgiven by a handful of wretched people who will soon, in any case, be extinct; whose main occupations are sleeping and picking their lice; and whose whim can decide the success or failure of his whole enterprise.

This complaint reminds us of Malinowski in his darker moods. Lévi-Strauss whose cast of mind always led him in the direction of philosophy, worried over the problem of values. If an anthropologist had to remain objective and accept the societies he studied without moral judgments, did it follow that he must remain uncritical of his own society?

At any rate, the society to which he returned was then embarking on the second devastating war which was to involve most of the western world. In 1941, after the occupation of France, he was invited to teach in the New School for Social Research of New York, thanks to American anthropologists (Lowie and Rhoda Metraux) who took an interest in his work and also to the Rockefeller Foundation's plan for the rescue of European scholars who might be in trouble under the occupation. Since Lévi-Strauss was Jewish, anything might have happened to him.

The problem was: how to get to the United States? He tried for a passport to Brazil on the pretext of continuing his studies, but his friend, the ambassador, was prevented by new regulations from renewing his visa. Lévi-Strauss had shared in the retreat of the French army, serving as a liaison officer between the French and the British. Now a concentration camp threatened him. Finally, he heard of a ship sailing for Martinique. It was a small boat and although he knew officials of the line, they first put him off telling him it would not afford comfortable accommodations. When he at last acquired a ticket, he discovered that this ship, with only two cabins, was carrying 350 passengers. Its departure reminded him of the sailing of a convict ship with police officers roughly separating the travellers from their friends. Among Lévi-Strauss's fellow passengers was the famous surrealist poet, André Breton, with whom he became friendly.

It was a miserable trip with inadequate sanitary facilities. When the refugees reached Martinique, they discovered, however, that most of the island population was collaborationist. The unfortunate refugees were treated as despised enemies and most of them interned. Lévi-Strauss was allowed to go ashore because the captain of the ship had been second officer on the vessel on which he had travelled to Brazil in the past. Unfortunately, Lévi-Strauss had brought with him countless files, journals of his travels, negatives, charts, filing cards and rolls of film. He felt sure that customs officials would assume that Indian vocabulary lists were spy codes and the plans, maps and photographs secret military information. Fortunately, he got his trunk on board a ship for Puerto Rico unopened by having it sealed and declared luggage in transit.

His troubles were not at an end, however, for when he arrived at Puerto Rico, the United States customs officials were as stupidly suspicious of his files as he had feared the Martiniquians might be. He was interned while the State Department decided on a French expert to inspect his belongings. This took three weeks. Then the first note card the F.B.I. man picked up was in German! It was explained to him that it was a note taken from the work of a famous nineteenth-century explorer of the Matto Grosso. Finally, the young man calmed down and the distinguished French scholar was permitted to enter the United States.

While in America, he met Roman Jacobson, a student of language, who was to have a profound influence upon Lévi-Strauss as a theoretician. Jacobson (borrowing from Ferdinand de Saussure, who wrote in 1910) had developed an approach to linguistics in which he studied the relationships between words. From his point of view, the object which the word designated, its meaning, was not important, but the patterns which the words formed, the grammatical relationships, were the essential basis of language. This "structuralism" treated language as a kind of mathematics. Lévi-Strauss was converted to Jacobson's method and proceeded to apply it to anthropology.

He taught in the New School until the end of the war. In the fifties he did field work in India and is now Professor of Social Anthropology at the Collège de France in Paris.

It is in the last two decades that Lévi-Strauss has produced a series of books, distilled from his field work data, which have placed him in the front rank of modern anthropologists. In these volumes he has attacked most of the major theoretical problems of his science and, although his ideas are controversial, they are certainly a distinguished contribution to scientific thought.

Basically Lévi-Strauss attempts to show that the mind of preliterate man does not differ in the way it works from that of the so-called civilized person. The most basic solution, and the most convincing, is his analysis of totemism.

Now totemism was a term used by anthropologists all during the nineteenth and early twentieth century. Early anthropologists felt that it was a semi-religious connection with animals which were considered to be ancestors. Anthropologists continued to study what they called totemism all over the world. Finally a gallicized Dutch scholar, A. van Gennep, in 1920, wrote a summary of the state of the problem, in which he listed forty-one different definitions of the word. The difficulty arose from the fact that, in many areas, clans or parts of tribes were named for animals or plants. Sometimes the two sexes were separated and each given the name of an animal or plant. Sometimes there were elaborate marriage regulations which insisted that people of a certain animal or plant totem had to marry a person identified with another specific totem. Sometimes a group considered itself descended from a totem. Sometimes there seemed to be individual totems. Sometimes a person was forbidden to eat his totem. Early scholars had tried to account for the fact that not all these ideas were present at the same time in each culture. They did think that there was some basic notion of a connection between human beings and the natural world. Some anthropologists thought that all early peoples had passed through a stage which they called totemic. But were all these different relationships to plants and animals really totemism? If not, then where did you draw the line? This state of confusion accounted for the forty-one definitions.

Lévi-Strauss took the position that the whole historical concept of totemism had only existed in the minds of anthropologists and their disagreements proved that there was no such institution, it was an intellectual concept. Instead, said Lévi-Strauss, one had to re-think all the elements and come up with a new approach to the preliterate mind. He found the germ of the solution in some notes by the English anthropologist, Radcliffe-Brown. In New South Wales, Australia, the bat is a male totem, the tree creeper belongs to the females. A characteristic in common was that both lived in holes, while one was a flying furred animal and the other a bird. Other such pairings could be seen in the eaglehawk and the crow, both carnivorous birds but the first a bird of prey, the second a carrion-eater. On this basis, Lévi-Strauss said that animal totems were not chosen because they were feared, admired, envied, or good to eat but because they were "good to think with."

Now, one of the weaknesses of early scholars had been their desire to see preliterates as inferior and different from the "civilized." They had therefore accused them of irrational superstition, child-like or "prelogical" attitudes. Lévi-Strauss insisted that a basic characteristic of all human thought was the urge to classify and to construct images of the world. Hence the preliterate was no different from his fellows in Europe except that his methods came closer to those of the poet than the scientist. The natural world was for him the source of a series of metaphors by which he could talk about his own social arrangements. The content of his thinking, the mythology by which he described the origin of or the reasons for what he did varied from place to place. The Australians might use the crow and eaglehawk, the American

Plains Indians the coyote and wildcat, but the structure of
their myths would reveal the same use of similarities and
differences in designating human groups in terms of natural
objects. This was the basis of the idea of totemism. The tabus
which were associated with animals, the marriage classes
designated by them, might or might not occur together in a
specific culture. The type of thinking about the natural world,
however, was universal.

Lévi-Strauss went further and, in his books analyzing South
American myths, he elaborated another characteristic of preliterate thought, the tendency to symbolize the apposition
between nature and culture and the transition from one to the
other. As Lévi-Strauss explained his basic typical myth, meat
exists so that man can cook it. The controlled fire used for
cooking is a symbol of man's relation to the sun: if the sun
were too far from the earth, the earth would rot and if it were
too close, it would burn. Cooking is an agent of passage from
nature to culture and the sun is the mediator between heaven
and earth.

Lévi-Strauss gathered hundreds of myths whose contents
seemed varied but by means of ingenious analysis proved they
could be reduced to his basic formulas. In the case of raw and
cooked, for instance, the puberty ceremonies which initiated
a girl into womanhood were thought of as "cooking" the raw-
ness of human nature. It must be admitted these reductions
of myth are not always convincing.

Thus Lévi-Strauss's approach to his subject is very much
that of an eighteenth-century philosopher. He searches for a
timeless formula which will cover the psychological facts, the
relationships he has recorded in myths and social structure.

There is, however, a basic contradiction in his personality
which appears in writing. His account of his field work in
Brazil, *A World on the Wane*, abounds in emotional insight
and sensitive reactions to the feelings of his preliterates. Yet

in his "scholarly" *Totemism* he writes "Actually impulses and emotions explain nothing; they are always results, either of the power of the body or of the impotence of the mind. In both cases they are consequences, never causes. The latter can be sought only in the organism, which is the exclusive concern of biology, or in the intellect, which is the way offered to psychology and to anthropology as well."

The division of body from mind is curiously old-fashioned thinking. It seems to state that there is a built-in formula for thinking in the brains of all men which has nothing to do with the personality of an individual and which shapes forms of culture without the need for great men or creative talents.

But rites, myths and ways of looking at the world do not arise miraculously from a group, they must ultimately be the creation of specific individuals, preliterate poets in short. It is nonsense to say that the emotions of such poets have nothing to do with the shape of their creations.

Lévi-Strauss's own observations contradict his theory. The poetic performance of the Tupi chief, which so impressed him, was certainly ecstatic and emotional. Even though the stories contained much inherited material, the emotional impulses of all the native poets of the past had a share in shaping the songs and dialogue of the folk opera.

One of Lévi-Strauss's sympathetic critics, Josselin de Jong, puts it this way: "We would like to point out that his structural view . . . . should be regarded as a dynamic factor in cultural patterning *by the side of unconscious collective drives and motives.*" The italics are mine. To divorce body from mind is a habit of which some modern thinkers are trying to rid themselves. Lévi-Strauss may be doing a service in emphasizing the intellectual motives in man's behavior but this should not be done to the exclusion of other elements which make up a living being.

Lévi-Strauss's structural approach has not only been taken

up by disciples of whom he thoroughly disapproves but has also been sharply attacked. A sociologist, Henri Lefèvre, wrote "He has a curious predilection, almost maniacal, almost schizophrenic, for the motionless, the diagram." The philosopher, novelist and playwright, Jean-Paul Sartre, with whom Lévi-Strauss disputes in print, calls his thinking reactionary because it denies change and seems to accept a closed world.

Actually there is no doubt that Lévi-Strauss is a split man. On the one hand, he is highly sensitive to sensuous detail and to emotional shadings and himself displays a romantic nostalgia for the simplicity and natural balance of the small vanishing cultures he has studied. On the other hand, his system makes man out to be a kind of mechanism responding to programmed circuits called structures and these structures supposedly arise, in some unexplained way, entirely from mental processes. Thus all cultures are at bottom patterns of mind filled with various kinds of content which are not in themselves significant.

Today, Lévi-Strauss gives twenty lectures a year at the Collège de France, a smaller and more intellectually select institution than the Sorbonne. An interviewer describes him as dapper in a hound's tooth leather sports jacket, a string tie with a silver clasp. His profile is narrow and aquiline, his hair white and bushy. Appropriately, his office is decorated with the feathered headdresses and the basket work of his Amazonian friends, friends, who since he left them, have been rapidly disappearing into the dark night of history.

Lévi-Strauss represents a trend in anthropology which sees the role of the scholar as similar to that of the zoologist or botanist. This school aspires to an analysis and classification of cultures which its members feel can become as exact as the mathematical science.

For our final study we turn to an American whose work takes a direction radically opposed to structuralism.

# 5

# MARGARET MEAD

Although anthropology, by definition, deals with man, the fact that women are a part of the human race often seems to be overlooked. It was not until the twentieth century that women became anthropologists. The best known of these in our time is the American Margaret Mead, and her apprentice period takes us into a decade when American anthropology made great strides, when the American school acquired a character of its own. Much of this progress was due to the influence of a great anthropologist and a great teacher, Franz Boas. Boas had spent a year (1883–4) among the Central Eskimos, a year of field work in which he lived in close contact with his informants and produced a comprehensive account of their culture and daily lives. He thus pioneered in the kind of study which Malinowski was to call functionalism and escaped from the museum approach of the European students of cultural traits. After spending a short time as Bastian's assistant in the Imperial Museum in Berlin, he returned on an expedition to the American Northwest. Circumstances provided him with a job on a magazine in 1887. He remained in the United States, worked eventually for the Field Museum of Chicago and the

American Museum of Natural History and, by 1921, was the head of the anthropology department of Columbia University. Never a nationalist, Boas was often attacked for his pacifist position during World War I, an attitude which made his position difficult at Columbia and resulted in story sessions in the Anthropological Society. Boas, a man of great courage and independent mind, weathered the storm and became the mentor of a whole generation of distinguished ethnologists, among whom were Alexander Goldenweiser, Robert Lowie, Melville Herskovitz, A. L. Kroeber, Edward Sapir, Ruth Benedict and Margaret Mead.

Boas had specialized in Northwest Indian culture. He collected many documents, developed the study of Indian languages and brought together most of the magnificent painting and carving which is displayed in the Northwest Indian Hall of the American Museum of Natural History.

Always wary of theory and speculation concerning the development of man's early cultural history, he emphasized the importance of collecting facts. He felt that the duty of his students was to do spade work and to help bring together a body of accurate source material upon which the science could build.

During Mead's student years the relations between her, Edward Sapir, Ruth Benedict and Boas were particularly close. In 1922, when Mead was a senior at Barnard, except for an adjunct course or two given by outsiders, Boas was the whole department. There were no undergraduate courses, all of the small graduate groups were taught by him. Mead wrote:

> Professor Boas, with his great head and frail body, his face scarred from an old duel and one eye drooping from facial paralysis, spoke with an authority and a distinction greater than I had ever met in a teacher. He believed in encouraging in his

students the very kinds of behavior which his authoritative and uncompromising sense of what was right and just tended to discourage. Characteristically, after a semester spent asking us rhetorical questions which we hardly ever ventured to answer— though I would write the answer down in my notebook and would glow with pleasure when it turned out to be right—he excused me and other students from taking an examination, because of 'helpful participation in classroom discussion.'

In a course involving measurement in physical anthropology he suddenly remarked that he was embarrassed. "Some of you do not know the calculus. I will teach you the calculus." In the twenty minutes left of the hour he did. In his lectures, Boas referred to tribes all over the world without placing them in time or space; he spoke with a strong German accent and gave references first in German, as an afterthought in English, expected his students to use reference works in Danish or Dutch, and prepared his lectures as if he were about to talk to a hundred of his peers. Eventually, the students in the department took the courses more than once because each time they were almost completely different. At this point, Boas was still interested in diffusion and made his students trace a trait or a theme from culture to culture, showing the changes which the trait or group of traits underwent. He would show, for instance, how a design element representing the gable of a house with a column-like element on either side would, in the course of travelling from the Northwest to the Pueblo area, become three rainclouds with rain falling from them. The student in this type of study had to read every scrap of relevant material, annotate, analyze and localize on maps. At the same time, in lectures, Boas never ceased to point out the error of attributing the origins, forms, or changes in human cultures to a single explanation. Boas had just promoted Ruth

Benedict to be his assistant and she, in turn, had just found that anthropology was a study which gave meaning to her life. Mead, who was taken by Benedict on field trips to the Museum of Natural History, found the older woman to be shy yet enthusiastic. Although she could not talk fluently, she was already able to communicate her excitement concerning the Plains Indians' Sun Dance. An introspective woman with delicately chiselled features, at this time Benedict always wore the same dowdy dress. When Mead asked for references in relation to the Sun Dance, Benedict blushed and brushed aside the request. When Mead persisted, it turned out that she was embarrassed at mentioning her own first published article, "The Vision in Plains Culture."

By the end of the first semester, Mead became so enthusiastic and talked so much about the course on the campus that the registration doubled. Toward Boas, who had a magnificent sense of man's development through the ages, Mead felt a sense of urgency because it was rumored this might be his last year of lecturing. She felt the need "to rescue the beautiful, complex patterns that people had contrived for themselves to live in that were being irrevocably lost all over the world. So I began to attend all the graduate courses, little groups of five or six students under a professor who had no time for administrative red tape and who was perfectly willing to let an undergraduate go where an undergraduate wished."

It is interesting to note that Mead herself, underlines the appeal to the imagination of preliterate cultures. Benedict had come to anthropology from the study of literature. Both she and Mead wrote poetry, as did Edward Sapir, the third anthropologist who was to contribute to Margaret Mead's development.

Sapir was born in Germany and was eventually to teach at Yale. Not only did he, Benedict and Mead write poems

they sent to each other, which sometimes were published, but
he was particularly interested in the new developments in
psychology called psychoanalysis.

Up to this point, in anthropology the emphasis had been
upon institutions, artifacts, broad lines of human development.
Although Malinowski showed some interest in psychoanalysis,
nevertheless in his work there was a tendency to shift the
emphasis away from the individual human being. In 1922,
Sapir was writing to Benedict, "I should like to see the problem of individual and group psychology boldly handled, not
ignored. . . ." Sapir had been reviewing books on psychoanalysis for a literary publication, *The Dial*, as early as 1917.
Margaret Mead herself also encountered this new trend when
she took a course with the sociologist, William Ogburn, at
Columbia, a course in which work by the three great names
in psychoanalysis, Freud, Jung and Adler, was discussed.

The question, therefore, now being asked in anthropological
circles was: what does the development of individuals have
to do with the character of their culture?

Now depth psychology, as formulated by Freud, stressed
the importance of the first few years of a child's life. Up to
his time, the child was considered to be an innocent angel or
a little devil and that was about all. But, said Freud, innate
in the child were certain drives or desires, a sex attachment
to the mother, a fear of loss if the parents neglected it, which
could cause anxiety and a sense of competition with the father
for the mother's love. How these drives were satisfied, rebuffed
or transformed, determined whether the adult became well-
balanced or neurotic, that is, emotionally disturbed and hard
to get along with.

In other words, if the average person in one society was
often angry and aggressive and in another gentle and peaceful,
it might be possible to find out how he got that way. Carrying

the idea further, it might also be possible to understand how the admirable and not so admirable traits in our own society came about.

In the very early twenties, these new psychological interests were merely in the talking stage. The kind of psychology which was generally dominant in this period has received the name of behaviorism. It owed a great deal to the experiments of the Russian Ivan P. Pavlov who worked with animals. He discovered that by repeatedly ringing a bell and presenting food to a dog, the dog began to secrete saliva. Finally, by merely ringing the bell, the dog secreted saliva. This was a basic principle which was extended later in experiments with small children. Living things could be trained to respond to whatever stimulus the experimenter chose to apply. This, of course, resulted in an attitude which treated the human being as a machine. Freudian psychology, however, developed the concept of the unconscious, an area of emotional and intellectual process, of which the individual was not really aware, but in which emotional patterns formed, symbols were created and combinations and choices went on in the brain. Dreams were symptomatic of this activity. It was a complicated idea and a very different picture of mental processes from the penny-in-a-slot version of the behaviorists. The Freudian thought that images and ideas from the unconscious could sometimes be made conscious and thus emotional difficulties could be cleared up. The behaviorists simply ignored consciousness; since it did not fit into their scheme they pretended it did not exist.

These two attitudes have persisted in psychology and we still do not know how to resolve them. In Malinowski's time, behaviorism influenced his thinking. On the whole he was not interested in the development of individuals. When Margaret Mead was ready for her first field assignment, she was already influenced by the psychoanalytical approach. She wanted to study adolescence because this was a period in young peoples' lives which seemed particularly full of problems. Educators believed that the process of coming into adulthood, the crisis of awareness of sexual maturity, was bound to be a point of emotional tension. This was when young people became moody, dreamy, self-conscious. They often felt rebellious because they thought their parents should no longer treat them as children. On the other hand, they were not really ready to face the responsibilities of grown-up living, and thus could not understand the importance of continuing their education. They sometimes became dropouts from school or, at worst, if their problems became too intense, even turned into delinquents. The educators considered all this storm and stress to be unavoidable. Mead's idea was to study the upbringing of a preliterate group during this stage of living, keeping in mind what went on in western civilization. Would there be differences? Perhaps adolescent anguish was not universal.

Boas was sympathetic to the idea, although he was no Freudian. Since his bias was toward American Indians, he favored an Indian tribe for her study. Mead, however, had done research in the library on the South Seas. Few Indian tribes retained much of their original culture. In the South Seas, she felt she might be able to find a group which had not undergone the influence of the West and which retained its ancient customs.

Her project provoked a mild crisis. For a young girl, just out of college, to take off for the South Seas, long publicized as a region of cannibals, was an unheard of idea. It is true that, in the twenties, women were beginning to assert their rights to take up many occupations not before open to them. Anthropology was something else. While Margaret Mead has never considered herself a feminist, nevertheless the impact of

her work and activities has helped to broaden the opportunities for women. She, herself, was in one of her books to undertake a comparison of male and female temperaments and
capabilities.

In any case, Boas, called by his students "Papa Franz," was
often an obstinate and patriarchal parent and, in this case,
objected strongly to the whole idea. An anthropologist had
been murdered in the South Seas and others had died of tropical diseases. Mead, however, set out to convince her family
that she was right. Fortunately, she had allies in this camp.
Her father was an economist, her mother a sociologist. Indeed,
the first wedding she ever attended was an Italian one, for her
mother was studying Italian immigrants in America. Thanks
to this social science background her family was won over.
Her father offered to supply the balance of funds necessary
for the trip if she could obtain a National Research Council
Fellowship.

With this backing, she went back to Boas and reproached
him for being a tyrant. Boas, who was really soft-hearted,
could not bear to see himself in the role of wicked stepfather
and gave in. He recommended her for the fellowship but
stipulated that she must choose an island at which a boat
stopped every three weeks. Samoa, of which little was known
at the time, seemed most practical.

Although picked more or less at random, the island was
an excellent choice for the study since the girls of this culture
received an upbringing radically different from that of western
civilization. Mead's Samoan project was a pioneering effort
from another angle. Until her time, a period in which there
were still few field workers, no woman had ever studied the
members of her own sex in a preliterate group and taken
advantage of the fact that she could gain information which
would have been impossible for men to obtain.

Although Mead actually lived in the house of the machinist's mate in the American navy base, like Malinowski she spent all of her waking hours immersed in the life of the village. Her focus was the group of adolescent girls, and from what she learned of them and of their relationships to their elders in three small villages she was able to create a picture of native life. In the nine months of her stay she learned the language and participated in the activities of the women. To do this, she had to shed her western habits. The Samoan sat cross-legged on the ground (a chair made her stiff and uncomfortable); she ate with her fingers from a woven plate; she slept on a mat on the floor, her neck supported by a bamboo headrest instead of a pillow. Coco palms, breadfruit, bananas and mangos swayed about the village. The houses were mere circles of pillars, roofed by a cone of palm thatch, the sides consisting of woven blinds. The only animals were the pig, the chicken, the dog and the rat. Samoans ate breadfruit, bananas and taro, a starchy root ground into paste, which more or less took the place of the potatoes eaten in other countries. To add to the vegetables, there was fish and wild pigeon, half-roasted pork and land crabs.

Mead adopted their habits, ate their food, went about barefoot, played games, learned their skills, and generally made friends with about fifty girls. She wrote,

> The life of the day begins at dawn, or if the moon has shone until daylight, the shouts of the young men may be heard before dawn from the hillside. Uneasy in the night, populous with ghosts, they shout lustily to one another as they hasten to their work. As the dawn begins to fall among the soft brown roofs and the slender palm trees stand out against the colorless gleaming sea, lovers slip home from trysts beneath the palm trees or in the shadow of beached canoes, that the light may find each sleeper in his appointed place. Cocks crow negligently, and a

shrill-voiced bird cries from the breadfruit trees. The insistent roar of the reef seems muted to an undertone for the sounds of the waking village.

The environment was similar to that studied by Malinowski but the peoples' habits were somewhat different. As the village woke up, babies cried and were given the breast. Young men stumbled toward the beach on early fishing expeditions. Girls giggled over love adventures which occurred during the night. Children were given lumps of cold taro when they demanded breakfast. Women carried piles of washing to the sea or set off inland to get materials for weaving. Pebbly floors of houses were swept with a long stiff broom. Old men sat about, twisting palm husks. Carpenters worked on new houses. Some families prepared to cook a large dinner with taro, yams and bananas and a pig stuffed with leaves. As the sun rose and the heat intensified, small children, playing with frangipani blossoms for pinwheels, crept into the shadow of the houses. The women, when they walked in the sun, carried great banana leaves as sunshades or wound their heads with wet clothes. Most of the village took a nap at midday. Perhaps a few adventurous children went off for a swim.

In the cool of the afternoon the boats returned. The young fishermen separated the "tabu" fish, those which must be sent to the chief. Men came back from the bush, dirty from field work, laden with yam. Kava, a slightly intoxicating drink, was served to groups of the men. Girls wore necklaces. Children played round games. Finally, in the flaming sunset, the last bather came up from the beach, the families gathered for their evening meal. After supper, some of the young people might dance. The old men gossiped and made plans. Fishing was sometimes done by torchlight. It would be midnight before all were asleep.

Since Mead's concentration point was adolescent girls, she studied the duties and privileges of this group. Up to early puberty the girls were entrusted with the care of the babies and very young children. The babies were nursed, whenever they cried for the breast, up to two years of age. After that, their small nursemaids had to see to it that they did not annoy their elders. They carried babies astride their hips or the small of their backs and trained them in the necessary avoidances. Since it was not customary to punish children except for a slap or two (brutality toward the young seems to be more common as a development of "civilization"), the nursemaids had to keep them amused so that they would not cry or get into trouble. This meant that the lives of young girls were extremely restricted. They did, however, form little gangs and managed to play together when the babies were quiet.

Samoans had a relaxed attitude toward their children. These were free to take up residence in any household considered part of the family. Consequently if they were annoyed or felt they had been unjustly treated, they often moved to an uncle or aunt's household and might stay there for any length of time.

When the girls were old enough to carry fairly heavy loads, the babies were handed over to their younger sisters and the adolescents began to learn adult tasks. They then acquired more freedom but they took on most of the drudgery which the modern American housewife rebels against. They cooked, they ran errands, they cleaned up the hut and made themselves generally useful.

Meanwhile their brothers had lived a relatively freer life although small boys of five or six formed teams to help their father or older brothers fish and hunt. The heavy work of building an oven with hot stones for baking was also the boys' job.

The girl nearing adolescence was also expected to become skillful in home industries. Most important of these was many types of weaving. Vegetable fibers are the basis of interior decorating and useful arts in general in the tropical world. The palm, the pandanus (a kind of low palm) the banana all yield material for mats and baskets. The girl had to weave strong baskets for fish, and larger ones which could be hung on the body to carry produce. The Venetian type of blinds which functioned as walls to the houses had also to be woven from palm leaves. Floor mats, which were large and cumbersome, demanded another skill. Food platters were woven of palm leaves in intricate designs, the inner banana fiber forming a decorative dark strand. Sleeping mats had also to be woven and finally an especially fine mat made from carefully treated pandanus fiber, one-sixteenth of an inch wide, was the girl's masterpiece and an essential article for her dowry when she got married. Such a mat might take a year or two to finish. Finally, there was the production of bark cloth, the material for skirts and loin clothes. This was prepared by cutting mulberry wands, peeling the bark and beating it until it softened after it was scraped by the adults. Adults generally drew or painted the pattern upon the cloth.

This was the education of the Samoan teen-ager. At the same time, during the period of adolescence, she was free to indulge in love affairs. These premarital activities were similar to those in the Trobriand islands. They went on up until seventeen or eighteen. (In this period of their lives there seemed to be a natural sterility for few became pregnant.) When more serious attachments took place, the girls married.

One important aspect of Samoan culture was the fact that it discouraged competition. All were expected to do well, but extreme ambition was frowned on. Thus there was no pressure to keep up with or outdo the Joneses.

Each group had a priestess who lived a ceremonial life. There were also certain chiefs whose position carried prestige but these offices were determined on the basis of lineage and, to some extent, through family intrigue.

A parallel with the education of the girls, the training of the boys was intended to prepare them to follow in their fathers' footsteps. In the unspecialized society of the girls everyone had to be a jack of all trades. The boys learned how to manage a canoe, how to plant taro and cut meat. They joined a loosely organized young men's society, called the Aumaga, which could always be drafted for group activities. When it came to crafts, the boy had some choice: that of becoming a house-builder, a wood carver (an artist), a fisherman, or an orator (equivalent to a poet). In all of these pursuits, however, he was not supposed to excel too noticeably. Actually the responsibility of a chief was often avoided. He had to associate with old men, watch over an extended family (as many as thirty), settle their disputes, arrange their marriages, and, in general, see to it that they were fed and housed.

In contrast to this rather conformist ideal, in one area individuality was encouraged and excellence never limited; this area was the dance. The Samoans danced more often than the Trobrianders, in individual parties, when guests were received, at weddings and ceremonial festivities. There was no formal teaching; young people imitated their elders, practiced their own steps and, at the informal parties, the very small children were called out first and encouraged to do their stuff. Ukeleles had been imported to accompany the voice, for in former times a bamboo drum had furnished percussion. The whole company generally joined in the song and clapped or beat on the floor with their knuckles. The words of the song often consisted of jokes at the expense of various members of the village. The performers wore flowers, shell necklaces, anklets and bracelets of leaves. Girls put on elaborate bark skirts and the older dancers rubbed their skin with coconut oil. There were several definite styles. The princess always danced in a slow dreamy detached fashion. Actually the movements were related to the hula which has been popularized for the tourists in Hawaii. In contrast, there was also an athletic comedian's style with much loud slapping of the naked portions of the body, leaping about, pounding on the floor and slapping of the mouth with the open palm.

Psychologically, Mead felt that the dance, which pushed even the youngest into the foreground in group affairs, was valuable in reducing shyness and in giving children a healthy outlet for their emotions and their egos.

The sum total of her study was the discovery that the answer to the question whether adolescence was a time in the life history of every girl child full of stress and conflict was "no." In Samoa, adolescence was not set off from any other period in growing up. If one girl grew tall sooner than the others she moved into the area of the heavier tasks. The girl who was not so mature physically at the same age remained involved in less mature occupations. The young people moved into sex relationships when they were ready, and sex was not surrounded with danger signals and an atmosphere of crisis. The penalty for this casualness was an absence of the ideal of romantic love. The whole culture, with its emphasis on a conformist average, was not geared to excess. Actually the three or four girls who did not fit in and who were generally in a state of conflict with people around them, were people whose temperaments were more emotional and demanding than the average. Very possessive toward their lovers, they showed an intense jealousy. These girls moved from one family dwelling to another, failed to settle down, and their chances of marriage were considered to be poor.

When Margaret Mead wrote her book about her Samoan field work, she included a chapter on the American educational system and its problems. She felt that the relaxed Samoan family, the absence of conflicting standards, the easy initiation into sex made for a childhood free from tensions. In American culture the families were small, the ties intense, the country as a whole was full of stresses and conflicting values and our school situations were mechanical, not allowing children to progress according to their individual rates of development.

In 1928, there was a good deal of optimism concerning the possibilities of change, and Mead's book made a profound impression upon psychologists and educators.

In a preface to the 1961 edition of the book, Mead looks back rather ruefully to the mood of optimism of the twenties. Two wars plus the rise of totalitarian systems of government had intervened since then. "In these thirty-five years the problems of human culture have not lessened but increased in intensity." The hopeful social scientists of the twenties did not realize how ingrained and selfish the habits of those in power would remain. Now, eight years later, it seems as if only violent change could improve our educational system and crisis after crisis shows that we simply do not apply the valuable insights that we already possess to our very imperfect way of life.

Margaret Mead herself remarks that her optimism was to be modified after she observed other primitives "fear-ridden and hungry and harsh to their children." The Samoans stood for a romantic glimpse into primitive life, a glimpse which seemed to indicate that civilization had much to learn from simpler cultures.

When she visited the Manus with her first husband, Reo Fortune, in 1928, her studies had entered a new phase. Her first book had shown that human nature was extremely flexible, that different cultures modified the basic drives in human beings in different ways. In the first flush of enthusiasm over her discoveries about the Samoans, educators began to feel that if children were brought up free of conflicts, all would be well. The situation among the Manus, a group of natives living on the Admiralty Islands off the northern coast of New Guinea, came as something of a surprise. In 1928, the 2,000 Manus were little influenced by western civilization. They built vaulted thatched huts on stilts in a shallow lagoon and their children were used to canoes and the water from the time they could toddle. The house floors were made of slats which sometimes parted and allowed babies to fall into the water. They were rescued immediately, but from birth they got used to clinging firmly to their mothers and fathers as they were hauled up and down ladders and across rickety verandas and as their parents paddled swaying canoes about the reef. If the canoe did capsize, the baby simply held on until it was righted. In this demanding environment the small children learned to handle their own bodies efficiently. They were encouraged to walk early; if they fell, no one wept over them. They had to get up and try again. It was no wonder that they were little athletes by the time they were five or six. By this age, from wading and imitating their older brothers and sisters, they had learned to swim, and as soon as they could swim they were given little five-foot outrigger canoes which they immediately learned to manage. All this was done without violence. There was simply a steady pressure to achieve and plenty of approval when the goal was reached.

Along with this picture of child training two other interesting facts emerged. The Manus, who were essentially ritual businessmen, were neurotic about private property. If children broke, destroyed or lost property, they were slapped, lectured,

shamed. The appropriation of someone else's goods was also
frowned on and monotonous warnings not to touch went on
from the time the baby could crawl. Yet, in contrast, there
was complete permissiveness in other areas. Children were
never taught to respect their parents, they often slapped them
or ignored commands to stop what they were doing, to come
when they were called, or to perform necessary errands.

On the whole, the children did little work. The girls took
over a few household tasks after about twelve, but aside from
this they were free to grow up independent. They were given
the choicest food, never had to obey their elders, except in the
matter of property rights and proper sexual modesty, about
which the Manus were in some ways extremely prudish.

Parents were different from those in Samoan culture. The
father was very loving toward his children but not toward his
wife. Often the father and mother competed for the child's
love. This situation, in turn, was the result of another fact of
adult Manus culture. Marriage, like many other institutions,
involved complicated financial transactions and exchanges
which often resulted in hostilities between the two families.
No thought of affection between husband and wife entered
into it. Periodic payments went on all during the couple's
married lives. What, among the Trobrianders, was a fairly
relaxed status-seeking through property became, among the
Manus, a grinding emphasis upon work, more trade alliances,
the building of bigger canoes, the accumulation of shells and
dog teeth currency. There was a continual obligation to pay
back goods advanced by the bride's family, to pay out goods
for the betrothal of younger brothers, the obligation to reach
the topmost standard of native wealth. Much of this sounded
like a parody of some of the worst qualities in American civilization. Also, like Americans, the Manus had little use for
artists. They were rich enough to buy the handiwork of their

neighbors. In ethical matters their code was as harsh as Puritan New England. The Samoans had no sense of sin, but the Manus culture was watched over by the skulls of grandparents fastened to the ridgepoles of their houses in carved bowls. These spirits took a dim view of South Seas human nature. Sexual sins, failure to make proper payments on debts, insubordination within the family, breaking of tabus—all such transgressions the spirits found everywhere and punished by visiting the culprits or their relatives with sickness. The will of these spirits was transmitted to mortals through seances carried on by certain female mediums who spoke with a whistling sound.

The typical adults in this society were ill-tempered, high-strung, quarrelsome, harassed people, always conscious of their debts, obligations and the supervision of their disapproving ancestors.

Significantly, dancing was not practiced a great deal except for a men's dance, which, curiously enough, defied the usual prudery. As the men danced, they boasted and shouted ceremonial insults. Such dances took place when there was a large display of wealth in payment between two groups related by marriage. Those who made the payment dared the other group to repay them. Those who received goods danced to show their defiant acceptance of the obligation to pay for them.

Into this hostile adult world came the athletic, cheerful, independent and, on the whole, cooperative children. With the acceptance of marriage and its responsibilities, they were soon turned into the harassed, tempestuous, peevish, quarrelsome characters who were the type produced by Manus culture. Since they were brought up to be aggressive, the emphasis on private property and the endless disputes over payments tended to spoil the sunniest disposition.

If Mead's Samoan experience gave encouragement to those

who felt that society might be changed by gradual evolution, hopeful that the influence of better educational methods would spread, the case of the Manus tended to strengthen the arguments of the revolutionary. Admiralty Island culture showed that the existing forms of society triumph in the end. And how can the forms be changed unless they are drastically challenged and broken up?

In actuality, the Manus did undergo a revolution, a revolution which swept over them from the outside. During World War II, when American armies were spread over the Pacific, the Manus suddenly came in contact with modern technology on a large scale. A million or more soldiers with a western, more or less democratic attitude, armed with all the scientific magic of their electrically-powered culture, showed these people for the first time what the rest of the world was like. Already Catholic missions had preached ethical values somewhat different from the code of the skull on the roofbeam. Also American movies and the example of Australian officials (the island was under Australian mandate) had showed that women were not so rigidly hedged in by tabus in other parts of the world. The really shattering experience, however, was the coming of the American army. The natives were swept up in the whirlwind of activities carried out by the gum-chewing, khaki-clad foreigners. Where before they had paddled canoes, now they were taught to drive trucks. They saw the great mechanical birds of the westerners: disgorging refrigerators, washing machines, even tanks and bulldozers.

Though all this was merely the side effect of one of the world's greatest orgies of slaughter, it had a constructive effect on the islanders. When Mead heard what had happened, she obtained foundation support to study this living laboratory of change. Here was an opportunity to find out at first hand how human nature was reshaped by a revolution. It was a priceless object lesson which might shed light on the increasingly grave problems of the western world which was now endowed with the power to destroy itself.

In 1953, she stepped ashore on the new site of Peri village. It was now built on land, American style, for the houses were of the same design and carefully lined up. When the noisy enthusiastic crowd gathered around her, she was greeted by a man in carefully ironed white clothes, wearing a tie and shoes, who explained he was the "council," an elected official. After this, a letter was handed to her which read, when translated,

> Dear Missus Markrit:
> This letter is to ask you whether you
> will help me teach the children.

It was signed with the name of the schoolteacher. Another official brought her a list of rules for child care he had drawn up and asked for her criticism and suggestions.

> Quite suddenly, that June evening in 1953, I knew that today all of us, the people of Peri and of the other Manus villages, the boys who had run my house for me twenty-five years ago, now tall mature men with households of their own, and the weight of office on their shoulders, lived in the same world.

How had all this happened? How had a simple fishing culture begun to struggle into literacy?

After the first shock of contact with the Americans, there was a strong reaction, a kind of revivalist emotional religion sprang up. Prophets announced to the people that they had visions of mystical cargoes arriving on planes and ships, bringing all the riches of modern civilization. This was called the "cargo cult" and spread over large areas in the South Seas; even in the mountains, the people built bamboo "radio towers" to signal their ancestors. To prepare for this millennium, the people flung their dog tooth and shell money, their dancing costumes, spears, pottery, all of their old life into the seas. This kind of emotional upsurge had happened among the Sioux Indians of North America after contact with the whites. It was, of course, a resurgence of old beliefs in magic and did not help the people to help themselves. Among the Sioux it only hastened their disintegration. The Manus were more lucky. An intelligent leader arose, who was able to guide his people toward modernity. He broke with Catholicism, which had not encouraged them to modernize, and tried to set up a code which he felt would cure their worst faults. He made anger the chief sin. He worked for the democratic process, organizing courts, village councils, schools, the philosophy of majority decision. He tried to unify the islands politically. He advocated the equality of women and abolished all the old hampering tabus and avoidances.

Paliau, the leader, was an interesting and gifted man. He had never gone to a mission school but had joined the police and had practically taught himself to write with the help of his fellow police boys. During the Japanese occupation, he had cooperated with the Japanese, a policy which had been recommended by the evacuating Australians but which nevertheless had been held against him. Paliau was a Manus on one side of the family, but actually lived on an island some distance from Peri. When he developed the "new way of thinking," he had had no contact with the Americans but was able to gather up some of the mystical enthusiasm of the "cargo cult" and transform it into an acceptance of a kind of town meeting democracy. He had succeeded in uniting thirty-three villages, but he was both supported and blocked by the Australians. The top officials helped him in a limited way, invited him to Port Moresby and taught him some organization methods but split up the territory over which he had control. Many of the lower officials and Australians with a confirmed colonial, racist attitude, however, did their best to slander and discredit him. They referred to him as a local Hitler, called him the "Emperor," said he had a huge harem of women and that he was served by a kneeling line of menials. They accused him of planning a totalitarian regime over an "empire," which was to include the Admiralty Islands, New Britain and New Ireland.

Margaret Mead found him to be a dignified, intelligent rather lonely man with a vision. The sea people were to have land, the land people were to learn to fish, his South Sea world was to develop the forms of modern European life and the inward virtues of the brotherhood of man, peaceful cooperation, shared resources.

To record all of these changes, which were occurring so rapidly among this people whose profile she had sketched twenty-five years before, Mead now used the motion picture camera and the tape recorder. What was happening to the Manus was symptomatically significant for, in the aftermath of World War II, colonies had been given independence all over the world, underdeveloped peoples not only in the South Seas but in the great African continent were all struggling with the problems of bridging a gap of four thousand years. How were they to adjust to the modern world and what kind of a modern world did they want? For centuries the peoples of the earth had been dominated by the white Europeans and now populations of another skin color were asserting their worth and dignity. Even in America (and soon the agitation was to become more intense) the Negro minority was beginning to assert itself in a new way. A different kind of balance in the human condition was being sought, whether the process was to be violent or, by intelligent guidance, peaceful and planned would be determined by man's use of the knowledge and insights already gained from the study of culture and group behavior.

Mead recorded a number of observations concerning Manus character, which she felt had to do with the flexibility of this people. The children she had observed twenty-five years before had been physically skillful, able to imitate adult activities to perfection. Thus, when they were confronted with the machines of the modern world, they were soon able to learn the techniques for controlling outboard motors or even bulldozers. But now, as she looked back, she realized that their play was remarkable for the fact that they never imitated adult social relationships. They never played at war, marriage, trading or death rites. In this they differed radically from the young Samoans. Mead now felt that this was a symptom of their dislike for the harassing world of restriction which would close upon them when they grew up. They shut it out. They pretended it did not exist. Often young men rebelled by running away and working in the plantations of the whites. She realized the potential of revolt already existed when the war changed everything.

> In retrospect it is possible to suggest that twenty-five years ago, the sense of an undesired, unlovable, and unfree future lay upon their youthful spirits much as the hopelessness of their future social position has been found to lie upon and depress children of partly acculturated native people or minority groups who, after a promising childhood, lose all incentive to use their minds or respond freely or imaginatively in school.

In other words, there was a parallel with our own dissatisfied or underprivileged young people. And indeed, the parallel can be carried further in the "dropout" attitudes of many of our slightly older groups who are in a state of rebellion against the world of their elders. The positive side of the picture was the eagerness with which young Manus, given constructive leadership, embraced a new way of life which they felt would result in a better society. And, of course, the implied question is, will our own youth achieve that leadership? The greatest irony was the fact that the westerners had abolished local warfare among the islanders but had not succeeded in outlawing it among themselves, and that a byproduct of our own technological slaughter had been the freeing of the Manus from their age-old fetters.

The story of the Manus is spread over many years. Another of Mead's studies takes us back to the thirties. It led her back to New Guinea and to the investigation of three simple cultures, not too far apart geographically (not over one hundred miles) but exhibiting remarkable differences.

The words "tomboy" and "sissy" are traditionally used in our culture. If we stop and think, we can see that they imply we know how a girl should behave and what a boy should be like. Any deviation from some vague mental picture of boyishness or girlishness therefore brings out these expressions of disapproval. Along with this go certain conventions in dress considered proper for one sex or the other. If we carry the ideas still further, we must realize that these stereotypes (as such conventional pictures are called) extend also into judgments of character connected with either sex. Whenever a man says, "Just like a woman!" he is automatically referring to a stereotype and not a very flattering one.

What Mead set out to do in her study *Sex and Temperament in Three Primitive Societies* was to sketch the portrait of men and women in these three cultures and to see if the accepted normal image differed. Once more, by forgetting about western ideas, it might be possible to learn something about what was masculine and what feminine.

The mountain Arapesh lived in isolated family groups which occupied a strip of land stretching from the seacoast over the mountains and down into the valley of the Sepik river in New Guinea. Those near the sea did a little fishing but were not at home in the water. Most of them tilled the scarce, infertile soil of the mountains. They did not think in terms of owning land, rather they belonged to the soil and cultivated it in small cooperative groups. The angle of the mountainside made fencing almost impossible. Wild pigs ravaged the gardens, and even the domesticated pigs were thin and razorbacked. Gardens were faraway, firewood was difficult to collect. In this culture of scarcity the relationship between mother and child was prolonged with a great deal of gentle play and warm bodily contact as the child was carried about in a sling so that it could often be given the breast. Arapesh boys were not encouraged to be aggressive. Injuring others was considered to be the greatest sin. Men were as responsible as women for the care of children and were as patient as women in holding, feeding and cleaning small children. Groups of Arapesh sometimes became involved in clashes with other hamlets but these were seldom serious. An argument would begin which turned into an angry quarrel; finally one of the aggressor group would throw a spear, being careful not to aim to kill. Someone would throw a spear back. When someone was finally wounded, the attackers all ran away. Later, peace would be made by exchanging rings. These people were not particularly creative; they got objects and artwork by trading with the coastal groups.

Both men and women in this mild-mannered group were gentle, sensitive, both sexes very much alike in personality. The aggressive members of the group were the ones who did not get along with their fellows. Some of these could be said to be neurotic.

The second group studied was the Mundugumor, a tribe which lived on a branch of the Sepik river and whose head-hunting and cannibalism had been prohibited only three years before when British control was implemented. This meant that their way of life was doomed. What Mead described was the culture as it had been and as it was still remembered. The Arapesh had warned her to be careful, they were still convinced that the Mundugumor ate people. Mead and her husband were chiefly concerned with recording the life of a people who had not yet been studied and hence they had to avoid two other groups who were being observed by other scholars. It was partly by chance that the Mundugumor were chosen. As it turned out a more interesting contrast could not have been arranged.

The Mundugumor were originally bush people who, when a small stream had turned into a river, found themselves obliged to copy canoes of their neighbors and to make a guarded use of the river but it seemed to Mead that they still feared it. Originally no member of the group ate someone who spoke his language. The rise of the river cut the people in two. They became so alienated that the tabu was dropped and they finally ate each other tranquilly. In no sense artisans, the Mundugumor bought woven baskets, hatchets and pots from their despised and tyrannized neighbors. The men, however, did carve fine warriors' shields, spears and also carved on triangles of bark used at yam feasts. This tribe was feared by all its neighbors because hostility was the key to their society. The men were polygamous and supposed to exchange their sisters for wives. Those who had no sisters had to take wives by force. Sons hated their fathers for they were harshly raised and often saw their mothers ill-treated, sometimes even beaten with a crocodile jaw. Then, too, because it was the custom for old and successful men to marry young women, there was fierce competition even between sons and fathers for the same woman. Both husband and wife detested pregnancy, fretted at the tabus surrounding it which decreed a period of no sex. Children had no prestige value and were not loved. Indeed, some at birth were bundled up in leaves and tossed into the river. While babies, they were hung up in uncomfortable baskets, and suckled only when their crying became unendurable. They were roughly weaned and brutalized in initiation ceremonies by being cut with crocodile teeth, burned or beaten.

The women in this culture were as hostile as the men. They did the hard work such as fishing and collecting coconuts while the men carried on rituals and hunted heads. Even the rituals had degenerated and were not held regularly but rather when some important man wanted to show off by giving a feast. Women were also as violent as the men in sex matters. Brief passionate affairs, which took place in the bush, were distinguished by much biting and scratching. A sign of love was to break each other's belongings; the girl broke her lover's arrows, the man destroyed her ornaments. All in all, the Mundugumor, in setting up a single violent angry type of individual as the norm, had created a culture that was the exact opposite of that of the Arapesh.

The third group studied, the Tschambuli, were a lake people who lived on a body of water connected with the Sepik river. Surrounded by small, sharp hills, the almost black waters of the lake were covered by pink and white lotuses and deep blue water lilies among which stood white ospreys and blue herons. In this charming setting, the Tschambuli built large ceremonial men's houses, mounted on high posts, on each of whose high gable ends a huge red and white face was carved in low relief, surmounted by a high thatched steeple ornamented by a wooden bird and the figure of a man.

These people lived on fish and sago and taro. Food was plentiful, the serious fishing and the hard work of the village done by the women. Children were brought up in a casual way and weaned easily. The boys, however, had to undergo a painful puberty ceremonial, which consisted of carving patterns in the skin of their backs. This scarification seemed to have lost its ethical, social or supernautral meaning and was merely an excuse for ceremonial. And ceremonial, for the men, was the whole of life. After the scarification ceremony, the boy was left to grow up an artist-performer, perfecting his dancing, painting or flute playing. Girls became solid citizens, fished, traded, carried on the domestic manufactures. The boy spent a good deal of his time in the men's house, working on ceremonial activities. Here there were complicated orders of rank and relationship, frequent quarrels and generally neurotic touchiness. Ceremonials took place constantly and involved masked dances, songs, the use of flute and slit gongs. Flute playing was highly specialized: the instrument could imitate a cassowary, bark like a dog or cry like a bird. A set of flutes blown together sounded like a pipe organ. Most of the theatricals were gotten up for the benefit of the women and involved sexy pantomimes in which the men sometimes played female parts, at other times the women joined in and courted them provocatively. The masks were fastened to bush headdresses of leaves and flowers into which dozens of delicate little carvings on sticks were thrust. Paunches were made of shells which extended below the waist like elephant tusks. On their rear ends, the performers wore bustles with carved faces fastened upon them. Their legs were covered with straw leggings. The figures sometimes came down from a raised stage with a backdrop suggesting mountains. The male masks carried spears, the female ones brooms. They sang songs through little bamboo megaphones.

Although men were nominally in control of the culture, Mead felt their temperament, coy, frivolous, flirtatious, was what we might ordinarily call feminine while the women, more aggressive in sexual affairs than the men, had many qualities that the West would associate with the male. The men, who were caught between an inherited tradition of male dominance and a reality in which they lived irresponsible lives, were often neurotic and given to hysterical outbursts. Really dominant men and passive women were the maladjusted people in this society.

The result therefore of this study of three groups was to show that even the popular notions of what was male and what female temperament were not based on absolute traits. Men and women's characters were molded by their culture and traits which we might call male or female could be imposed on either sex. Mead subsequently wrote a book on male and female stereotypes in America which drove this point home. And indeed, in recent years the changes in clothes and hair style among young people have tended to blur many of the traditional differences in this country.

Margaret Mead has written other books and made various contributions to educational psychology but the work in the South Seas created the personality and culture school of anthropology. Its importance for the development of the study was its emphasis on the process of change and upon the possibility of ferreting out the reasons for certain kinds of character and behavior. If, by a comparative study of groups, we could find out why we do what we do, we might be able to control the future and even avoid the destructive behavior so prevalent in the national and international scene.

Mead's work is an answer to the pessimistic belief that "you can't change human nature." Granted that certain basic animal appetites are always present and that certain processes of the mind are universal, man's forms of expression certainly vary and can be changed. We must first begin by being distrustful of all vague generalizations inherited from the past. Our images of maleness and femaleness are a good example. The lesson to be drawn from the story of Manus tells us something about change. The appearance of Paliau at just the right time probably kept his people from extinction. Mead stresses the fact that he knew just enough of the West to give him a goal toward which to work, but he did not suffer from the over-complication of a college education which might have con-fused him by alienating him from his people and prevented him from acting. His intelligence plus a gift for vivid figures of speech made it possible for him to convince groups of his compatriots. Added to this was the character of the young people who were already in revolt against the past when Paliau came among them. Finally the emotion of the cargo cult had swept away belief in the old ways and made it much easier for Paliau to spread his new doctrine.

There is hope that the more we understand the conditions for change, the more we shall be able to produce it and con-trol it. In all of her work, Margaret Mead has always shown an interest in education, in the value of anthropological knowl-edge for our lives today.

A short, sturdy woman of boundless energy, in her office perched high in the tower of the American Museum of Natural History, where she is curator, she has produced a steady stream of books and articles interspersed with her many field trips to the South Seas. Indeed, her description of field work glows with an enthusiasm which is infectious:

Most of all we like to spend our lives on field trips, away from offices and laboratories and storerooms, out somewhere collecting materials, making new photographs, learning new languages. There is always a temptation to take a new field trip before the last has been properly written up and to put off until later the tedious task of classifying what we have already brought home from the field. The mere suggestion that a new field trip might be possible sets an anthropologist to sniffing the air for remembered smells of fish oil, copra, roast tapir or chewed betel nut.

Although she, too, stresses the importance of recording the details of simple cultures before they disappear forever, she feels that anthropologists will be needed in the future, "to help human beings live without war on one planet. Their knowledge will be needed to feed and clothe and shelter billions of people living on earth in ways that will give them a better chance, each one to be what he has the potential to become."

# POSTSCRIPT

We have ended with two scholars who represent contrasting points of view. Lévi-Strauss's is that of the academic tradition and stems from the belief that science must remain "pure," that it must investigate for the sake of investigation. This is a defensible position and has resulted in valuable contributions to the sum total of human knowledge. It need not, however, be rigid and dogmatic.

Mead, and those who think like her, feel that the social scientist cannot remain indifferent to our most pressing and threatening human problems. The detached scientist feels he has no right to manipulate his fellow men, even for their own good. The applied scientist says men are already being manipulated by unscrupulous politicians. Perhaps the knowledge gained from our work can act as a counterbalance to passion and prejudice.

It is interesting and significant to compare a series of essays which came out of the 1967 plenary session of the American Anthropological Association dealing with *The Anthropology of Armed Conflict*. All of the essays but one are prudently analytical concerning the functions of warfare. Only Mead tackles a practical question, "Alternatives to War."

As Abram Kardiner, a well-known psychologist who had worked with anthropological material wrote in 1963, "Despite her prodigious efforts and ceaseless productivity, Mead could not buck the tide of conservatism in her own discipline." She brought psychology into anthropology in an effort to understand how people functioned in a group and, says Kardiner, this "invasion, as it was regarded in the early nineteen thirties, by psychodynamics resulted in a neglected dimension of the study of man, namely man."

When the present writer published his history of social anthropology in 1958, *From Ape to Angel*, he ended on a note of hope that this science might take the lead in contributing to improved social behavior in the world. Apparently he was overoptimistic.

A correspondence with Mrs. Miriam Camp Bradley, an anthropology student at the American University of Washington, D.C., is an interesting case in point. After having read my book, she wrote wondering why anthropology was not helping in our current difficulties. I replied, suggesting that she write to the NAACP and other organizations querying them on why no anthropologists were involved in easing racial tension. I also said that I felt they should have been active in various minority situations, such as the Puerto Rican problem in New York, and should be used continually in the State Department to help better understandings between peoples and to advise against such insanities as the war in Vietnam. I also suggested that she query her own instructors. On June 17, 1968, she wrote me, enclosing a reply from the NAACP which ran:

> This is in reply to your recent letter, and it is to advise you that the NAACP does not employ anthropologists in any capacity. This has nothing to do with our opinion of the value of anthro-

pologists in their sphere, but it simply reflects that we have no programs at present in which anthropological research or writing is relevant.

In her letter, she said "I also discussed the lack of consultation with anthropologists by various segments of the population and wondered why they just didn't come out and say here we are, may we consult with you. But the American University professors I spoke with said they would have to be *invited* to step up."

This interchange is saddening. Anthropology started out with such a wide field, with the possibility of its becoming a master science in the social area, that it would be a pity if it became just another dusty discipline in the halls of academe. Besides, in the light of the perilous situation of the world today, can social scientists afford to remain detached when the very survival of man trembles in the balance?

# BIBLIOGRAPHY

Below is a list of the books and other published works by the anthropologists covered in *Explorers of Man*. Since Adolf Bastian's work is available only in German, none of these are included.

HENRY ROWE SCHOOLCRAFT

*Algic Researches*, 2 vols. New York, 1839.

*Alhalla; or the Lord of Tallagega, a Tale of the Creek War with some selected miscellanies chiefly of early date.* New York, 1843.

*Expedition to Lake Itasca*, ed. by Phillip P. Mason. East Lansing, 1950.

*Historical and Statistical Information Respecting the History, Condition and Prospects of the Indian Tribes of the United States*, 6 vols. Philadelphia, 1855–57.

*Letters and Documents in the Smithsonian Collection of the Library of Congress.* Washington, D.C.

*Narrative Journals of Travels through the Northwestern Regions of the United States.* East Lansing, Michigan, 1953.

*Notes on the Iroquois.* Albany, New York, 1847.

*Oneota: The Indian in his Wigwam.* New York, 1944.

*Personal Memoirs of Thirty Years' Residence with the Indian Tribes.* Philadelphia, 1851.

*Plan for the Investigation of American Ethnology.* New York, 1846.

*Travels in the Central Portion of the Mississippi Valley.* New York, 1925.

"A Trip to Lake Superior," *Knickerbocker* magazine, XIII. New York, 1858.

*A View of the Lead Mines of Missouri.* New York, 1819.


## BRONISLAW MALINOWSKI

*Argonauts of the Western Pacific.* London, 1922.

*Coral Gardens and Their Magic.* London, 1935.

*Crime and Custom in Savage Society.* London, 1926.

*A Diary in the Strict Sense of the Term.* New York, 1967.

*Magic, Science and Religion.* Glencoe, Illinois, 1948.

*Natives of Mailu,* Transactions and Proceedings of the Royal Society of South Africa, vol. 39. Adelaide, Australia, 1915.


## CLAUDE LÉVI-STRAUSS

*A World on the Wane.* New York, 1961.

*Elementary Structures of Kinship.* Beacon Press, 1968.

*From Honey to Ashes.* Paris, 1966.

*The Savage Mind.* Chicago, 1968.

*Structural Anthropology.* Basic, 1963.

*Totemism.* Boston, 1968.

*Tristes Tropiques: Anthropological Study of Primitive Societies in Brazil, (II).* Atheneum, 1964.

MARGARET MEAD

*An Anthropologist at Work: Writings of Ruth Benedict.* New York, 1959.

*Anthropologists and What They Do.* New York, 1965.

*Coming of Age in Samoa.* New York, 1928.

*Continuities of Cultural Change.* New Haven, 1964.

*Growing Up in New Guinea.* New York, 1930.

*New Lives for Old.* New York, 1956.

# INDEX